Religions and the Status of Women

Status of Women Series

Religions and the Status of Women

Edited

Jyotsna Chatterji

A Joint Women's Programme Publication

UPPAL PUBLISHING HOUSE
New Delhi - 110002

UPPAL PUBLISHING HOUSE
3 Ansari Road, Daryaganj, New Delhi-110002

For
William Carey Study and Research Centre
14/2 Sudder Street, Calcutta 700 016
and
Joint Women's Programme

ISBN 81-85024-67-7

Printed in India
Published by UPPAL PUBLISHING HOUSE
3, Ansari Road, Daryaganj, New Delhi 110002
and Printed at Mehra Offset Press, New Delhi

JWP PUBLICATIONS

Status of Rural Women in India	75.00
Status of Nurses of India	60.00
Status of Women in the Quran (Urdu)	5.00
Status of Single Women in India	125.00
Status of Banjara Women	125.00
Trafficking in Women and Children in India	125.00
Women in Organised Movements	45.00
Child Labour in Bangalore City	30.00
A Socio-Economic Survey of Slum Dwellers in Calcutta	15.00
Women's Decade (An Assessment)	30.00
The Problem of Dowry in Bangalore City	5.00
Indian Women in Media	12.00
Women and Law	5.00
Prostitution with Relegious Sanction (Devadasi/Jogini)	20.00
Changes in Christian Personal Laws	3.50
Christian Marriage and the Customary Practices in Manipur	15.00
The Shahbano Controversy	125.00
Women in CNI Diocese of Delhi	5.00
Wake Up and Live!	5.00
Female Sexuality in Hinduism	
Women's Participation in Politics & Political Parties (Hindi)	250.00
Women in the Freedom Struggle (Hindi)	

Contents

INTRODUCTION

Religions and the Status of Women

JYOTSNA CHATTERJI*

In the Indian society which consists of many communities professing diverse religious faiths, religious tradition becomes of paramount importance in understanding the relative status of women and men. Religion has provided the ideological and moral basis for the status and role of women in society. The people's notion about the proper role of women in the home and society and the social restrictions on women are all rooted in religious conceptions regarding women. Each religion has its own myths and legends which emphasise the position of women.

That religious scriptures and sacred texts have influenced the status of women is an undeniable fact. In Christianity for instance, the creation story as found in Genesis 2 is often used to justify the low status of women. A few of the Old Testament stories and some portions of the Pauline writings emphasising the weak nature of women have so influenced the Christian community that even today the bias against women is prevalent both in the Church and in the community.

In Islam the same bias is visible. The recent case of Shah Bano, in which the Supreme Court granted this 70 year-old woman maintenance, led to protest movements by Muslim groups all over the country on the ground that the law of the Shariat prohibits Muslim women from demanding maintenance after divorce.

In the Hindu scriptures also we find texts that have conditioned the minds of people to such a great extent that even today the attitude towards women remains unchanged. A woman has been considered as the female principle complementing the male principle only when in union with the male. Separate from the male she becomes a dangerous and destructive force. Thus she is to be subjugated and controlled as a child, as a wife and as a mother.

---

*Mrs Jyotsna Chatterji is Associate Director of the Joint Women's Programme

The same attitude towards women persists today, thus making it impossible for women to live and develop as total human persons, capable of leadership and decision-making roles. For the Joint Women's programme (JWP) of the CISRS and WCSRC these factors arising out of religion were no mere academic questions but problems in its organising work. At the same time the JWP was convinced that the so-called religious obstacles were a result primarily of inadequate and incorrect interpretation of the religions. They felt it was necessary therefore to initiate a discussion on the relationship of the religions and the status of women today.

The Consultation on the 'Authority of the Religions and the Status of Women' held in Bangalore heard several papers on the various religions. These papers are included in this book. Academicians, religious leaders and members of social organisations who participated in this Consultation came to the unanimous conclusion that while all religions in their scriptures accorded some status to women, discrimination emerged in practice due to improper interpretation of the scriptures by those who preached the religion. The misinterpretations and the discriminatory texts led to unjust personal laws which needed to be studied from the point of view of human rights. They needed to be changed and rewritten to suit the spirit of the scriptures.

The Consultation stressed the need for a campaign to reform the personal laws of the various communities which discriminate against women, e.g., the abolition of the three *talaqs* in one sitting and polygamy in the Muslim personal law.

The Consultation also stressed the need to view the positive aspects of the religions and to use them to establish right relationships in society. The Consultation urged the participants to help in identifying the discriminatory and derogatory practices against women and work towards their removal so that women could claim their rightful status in society.

CHAPTER I

Femaleness: The Hindu Perspective

RANJANA KUMARI*

The concept of femaleness in Hinduism presents a duality. On the one hand the female is seen as divine, creative, nurturing and supportive and on the other, she is considered to be the epitome of what is dangerous, carnal and evil and, therefore, in constant need of control and subordination by man. Hindu religious texts abound in opinions about woman who is simultaneously seen as creative/good and destructive/evil. She is consequently both elevated and devalued.

The female is first of all divine, holy and pure and, therefore, worshipped. In Hinduism creation starts with Godhead which is conceived as a unity containing both male and female principles. Brahma, the Creator, is supposed to be half male and half female. At the moment of creation Brahma causes his body to separate into two distinct parts: *purusha* (male) and *prakriti* (female), and it is the union of this male and female principle which leads to creation.

> The lord (*Prabhu*) dividing his own soul (*atman*) and body (*deha*) becomes half male and half female. (*Manu*, I, 32)
>
> Verily, he had no delight. Therefore one alone has no delight. He desired a second. He was indeed as large as a woman and man closely embraced. He caused that self to fall (*pat*) into two pieces. Therefrom arose a husband (*Pati*) and a wife (*Patni*). Therefore, this is true: 'Oneself (*sva*) is like a half fragment' as Yagnavalkya used to say. Therefore, this space is filled by a wife (*Brihad—Aranyaka*, 1.4.3; cited in Pinkham, 1941: 68).

Some hold there is one Brahma, the emblem of eternal light. Others hold Brahma is of two kinds, *Prakriti* and *Purusha*. Those who hold that Brahma is one maintain that Brahma is the cause of all and transcends both *Prakriti* and *Purusha*, both of whom emanate from Him; or they maintain that the same Brahma wilfully divided Himself into two

---

* Dr. Ms. Kumari has been studying Female Sexuality in the Hindu Religious Tradition for the Joint Women's Programme of the CISRS and WCSRC.

parts... *Purusha* is eternal and so is Goddess *Prakriti*... They are parents of the world. (*Brahma Vaivartar, Krishna Janma Khanda*, 43, 56-67: Sen, II 293-294).

Woman along with the male is seen above as a direct emanation from the divine body and is thus a part of his divine self. The female shares the original divine power of Lord Brahma, and therefore feminine power is divine power.The spiritual equality of man and women is thus established. Another observation one could make is that the feminine principle is creative. When *prakriti* conjoins with *purusha*, it results in the creation of the world. The male and female unite in a harmonious union to create the world. Manu says:

> By the sacred tradition, the woman is declared to be the soil, the man is declared to be the seed; the production of all corporeal beings (takes place) through the union of the soil with the seed. (*Manu*, IX, 33).

Woman is thus seen as the yield or earth into which man sows his seed. She is the necessary receptacle of man's seed. She thus represents fertility and growth, and is the medium through which man realises himself. In mythology, this union is often represented by the union of Siva with his *Shakti* Parvati. The following extract illustrates this:

> Siva is man and Parvati is woman, they are the causes of creation. All men have Siva as their soul, and all women are Parvati. Siva has the form of the male sign (*linga*) and the Goddess has the form of the female sign (*yoni*). ; the universe, moving and still, has the form of the sign of Siva and the Goddess.... (*Brahaddharma Purana*, cited in O'Flaherty, 1975: 262).

Thus in the mythological formulation of Hinduism the female is seen as complementing the male to create. She is necessary to nurture man's seed and without her life is not possible. Symbolically too, the religious texts refer to her as *Archangini* his half-body, a part of man. In this way, as a divine as well as a creative power the female is deified.

However, this power is seen as creative and benevolent only when it conjoins harmoniously with the male. Separate from the male, in itself, her power is seen as dangerous and malevolent. In Hindu mythology the feminine principle, not conjoined with the male and not under his control, is represented as Kali, the symbol of irresistible power and chaotic energy which may be dangerous.

Watts (1969) explains :

> Kali is the embodiment of the Terrible Mother, the Spider Woman, the all-devouring man of the abyss, image of everything of which the human soul seems ultimately to be afraid. On the other hand she is eternal womanhood, cherishing mother of the world.
>
> (Watt, 1969: 84)

The belief that this power is a potentially a destructive force when unrestrained, that is when not under male control, is reflected in the popular myth of Goddess Kali performing her famous victory dance after killing a giant demon. In a bloody rampage she kills and destroys everything in her path without any control. Even the gods are unable to make her desist. When Siva, her husband, is sent to restrain her, he lies down at her feet. Kali, entranced by her killing, does not notice him and is about to step on him when she realises it is her husband and stops her rampage. Thus, when her husband regains control over her, the earth is saved. Kali is thus the embodiment of destructive power when unrestrained, but when under the control of her husband she is subdued. The benevolent goddesses in Hinduism are those who are married and who have transferred control of their sexuality to their husbands (Wadley, 1976). Thus a female deity under the control of a divine male transmutes into a benevolent being, and the male becomes the dominant member of the pair:

> As Parvati, Lakshmi, Sita or Savitri, she becomes a benevolent Goddess, a giver of wealth and progress, an exemplar of passive devotion to her husband.
>
> (Babb, 1970:141)

In other words the restraining social relationship of marriage subdues the dangerous force of the female. In religious symbolism a married woman thus undergoes a basic transformation—from a dangerous species to a loving wife, the source of wealth and happiness. Thus the male acts as a restraining factor and becomes supreme by subordinating his female *shakti* in marriage.

Hinduism thus presents a conception of the world in which female power is seen as divine and consequently worshipped. She is also worshipped as a creative and benevolent power when she complements harmoniously with the male, and when the male controls and subdues her. Consequently, unrestrained female power is seen as dangerous and malevolent.

It is against this background of the essential nature of femaleness that the Hindu ideal of womanhood can be derived. Religious texts consist of both explicit statements of proper behaviour for women as well as depictions of female characters who serve as potential models for desirable or undesirable womanly behaviour. In both these the predominant theme is that man must control woman and her power. The feminine religion, according to the scriptures, is to look upon the husband as a God, to hope for salvation through him, to be obedient to him in all things, never to covet independence, never to do anything but that which is approved by him.

The basic rules for women's behaviour excerpted from different religious texts stress the need to control women because of the evils of female character. Woman by nature is considered to be a deceitful and wily creature. She is deprecated in the following words:

> With women there can be no lasting friendship; hearts of hyenas are the hearts of women.*(Rig Veda, 10.95.15)*

> Truly there is no friendship with women, and theirs are the hearts of hyenas (*Satapatha Brahmana,* 11.5.1.9 cited in Pinkham, 1941: 61).

> (A woman) is the embodiment of rashness and a mine of vices. She is hypocritical, recalcitrant and treacherous.... she is an obstacle to the path of devotion, a hindrance to emancipation.... she is practically a sorceress (a magician) and represents vile desire. (*Brahma Vaivarta, Prakriti Khanda* 16.52-60, Sen, I, 132-133.)

> Falsehood, vain boldness, craftiness, stupidity, impatience, greed, impurity, and harshness are the natural qualities of women. (*Devi Bhagavata,* 1.5.83; *Vijayananda,* p.17.)

These observations make out woman as being born with evil inclinations and, therefore, all failings like craftiness, vanity and wickedness are seen as her natural endowments. According to The *Mahabharata* the vices and faults of women were so many that a man would find it inadequate even if he had a hundred tongues, lived for a hundred years and did nothing else but narrate all of them. Among all her vices, her sensuality came in for the sharpest rebuke.

Woman's role as a seducer of men is stressed and she is compared to the gateway to hell. She is accused of being lascivious, devoid of love for her husband and always tempting men. Her traits of inconsistence and fickleness were emphasised. The following extracts from different religious texts reflect this:

> Women do not care for beauty, nor is their attention fixed on age; (thinking) it is enough that he is a man, they give themselves to the handsome and the ugly....
>
> *(Manu, IX, 2)*

> Through their passion for men, through their natural temper, through natural heartlessness, they become disloyal towards their husbands, however carefully they are guarded in this (world). (*Manu.* IX, 15).

In The *Ramayana* woman is described as unstable and restless:

> This hath been the nature of the fair sex from the commencement of creation, that they gladden him that is well off, and forsake a person in adversity. And women imitate the instability of lightning, the sharpness of weapons, and the celerity of the eagle (*garuda*) and the wind.
>
> (*Aranya Khanda*, 3:13; Dutt, II, 535)

The dangers of women's love are explained in The *Puranas*:

> The three kinds of wine are called *Gaudi*, the *Paishti* and the *Madhvi*, the fourth sort of wine being the woman. It is the wine of woman's love alone that can intoxicate the three worlds. Wine, only when drunk, produces intoxication—whereas a woman, simply being looked at may madden the senses of man, and enshroud his consciousness in the darkness of nescience. Hence a man should refrain from even beholding a woman, as she is wine to his eyes.
>
> (*Agni* 353, 9-15; Dutt, II, 1301)

The same idea is reiterated in The *Puranas* and both the epics, The *Ramayana* and The *Mahabharata* :

> The father of a woman shall protect her in her infancy ; the

husband, in her youth; and her son, in her old age ; in absence whereof the duty of maintaining her shall devolve upon his friends and relatives.(*Garuda*, 95; Dutt, p.27)

The slave, the son and the wife, (these three) are always dependent. They can have no wealth; for, whatever they possess belongs to their master. (*Mahabharata, Sabha Parva*, 2.17.2; Dutt, II, 94.)

One of the refuges of woman is her husband. A second is her son, and a third is her relatives; and a fourth she has none. (*Ramayana, Ayodhya Khanda* 2.61, Dutt, I, 362).

The dependence of women on man is total and absolute, and if they dare break through these bonds of control, they are severely punished. Manu even allows man the liberty of beating his wife if she dares disobey him. Moreover, these religious texts frightened woman into submissiveness by very vividly describing the hell-like existence she would have to lead in her future life, if she dares to disobey her father or husband in this life. Manu has said :

By violating her duty towards her husband a wife is disgraced in this world; (after death) she enters the womb of a jackal, and is tormented by diseases, (the punishment for her sin).(*Manu*, V, 165)

It was because of such inherent weakness in the nature of womankind itself, that the religious literature prescribed control and subordination of women. Woman's sexuality is seen as dangerous and, therefore, the religious texts lay down very strongly that a woman should always be protected by a man and never given independence. Woman should be protected through all the stages of her life, and the ideal woman is the one who does not strive to break these bands of control. Says Manu :

By a young girl, by a young woman, or even by an aged one, nothing must be done independently, even in her own house.

In childhood a female must be subject to her father; in youth to her husband, when her lord is dead to her sons. A woman must never be independent.(*Manu*, V, 145)

In The *Puranas* the wife, whom a husband considered ideal to have in his home, is pictured in considerable detail :

> She who speaks sweetly to her husband and is a clever manager of household affairs, is a true wife. She who is one in spirit with her lord, and devotes her whole self to his happiness, is a true wife.
>
> He whose wife decorates her person with sandal paste, and perfumes her body after her daily ablutions, talks little and agreeably, partakes of small quantities of food, is very fond of him and is constantly engaged in doing acts of piety and virtue with a view to bring happiness and prosperity in the house, and is ever ready to yield to the procreative desires of her lord, is not a man, but the lord of heaven.(*Garuda* 108; Dutt, p. 350)

Noteworthy is the use of the word 'lord' to refer to the husband. A woman's husband is her lord, and it is her religious duty to see that he is happy and comfortable by yielding to every wish of his. The woman is defined primarily in relation to her husband and her household, and her interest and active participation in domestic matters is expected of her. The role of wife and mother is the optimal, singular and essential role through which a woman fulfils herself.

Thus an ideal woman is one who is submissive, dutiful, loyal and totally dependent upon her husband. Chastity is the most important component of the wife's behaviour. All the religious literatures have written about the glory, fidelity, and chastity of a married woman. Chaste women are referred to as *pativrata* and even supernatural powers are ascribed to them on account of it. In The *Mahabharata*, Bhishma described the anecdote of Sandili who attained divinity not through performance of any religious rites or penance but through fidelity and loyalty to her husband. She was always attentive to her husband and whatever he did she did. Any food or drink that he disliked she avoided, and when she was away from home she gave up cosmetics. Meanwhile, she kept herself busy with various auspicious activities and when he came back, she served him with rapt attention. She did all the household work and worshipped gods, forefathers and the Brahmana. In this way by executing all her conjugal and familial responsibilities dutifully, she attained divinity.(*Mahabharata, Anu*, 124)

The ideal of Sita, the heroine of the epic *Ramayana*, is placed before every Hindu girl. Sita's story emphasises the fidelity and chastity of a Hindu woman. She is worshipped as an ideal woman, uncomplaining, and a silent sufferer. The story of *Ramayana* revolves round the capture of Sita by the demon Ravana and the battle that follows between Rama and Ravana with Rama emerging victorious.

Sita, forcefully separated from her husband and in the clutches of the demon, is forlorn. She starves her body with the most severe kind of asceticism and remains pure both in body and soul. Even when incessantly assailed by the demon, she is immovably faithful to her husband Rama. Despite her fidelity and chastity, Rama publicly announces his suspicion of her character and refuses to accept her as his wife and humiliates her as she had lived with a strange man. Rather than question the justification of her husband's conduct or waver in her loyalty to him, she willingly subjects herself to a test of her purity of mind and soul. She jumps into a pyre and comes out unscathed, establishing her purity and chastity. Sita is wholly the Indian ideal of a woman, devoted, sincere, faithful and in the case of defending womanly virtue, noble in soul and pure in the body. Many beautiful appellations are given to Sita in The *Ramayana*. She is called :

'O Stainless one'	(5.56, Dutt, II, 1056)
'O noble lady'	(5.56, Dutt, II, 1057)
'Worshipful dame'	(5.34, Dutt, II, 986)
'Illustrious wife of Rama'	(5.58, Dutt, II, 1068)

All emphasise her chaste nature and the unceasing devotion of Sita to her husband.

Yet another ideal put up before Indian women is that of Savitri, who travels to the world of death with her husband's body, and through perseverance, and by being good and faithful, gets her husband's life back. Goddess Parvathi attains the distinction of a chaste woman because she does not tolerate the character assassination of her husband by her father. She prefers death to hearing it with her ears, and therefore she jumps into a lighted pyre and immolates herself.

All these stories reaffirm the deep-seated Hindu conception that a husband is a woman's greatest deity and she should worship him whatever his failings and shortcomings.

> Though destitute of virtue, or seeking pleasure (elsewhere) or devoid of good qualities, (yet) a husband must be constantly worshipped as a God by a faithful wife.(*Manu* V, 154)

> To a woman, her husband constitutes her God. The husband is a as pure as the gods, and represents all virtue.(*Brahma Vaivarta, Krishna Janma Khanda*, 57.15-25; Sen, II, 329)

> The sacred and imperative duty of a wife is to carry out the commands of her husband, and to live in perfect obedience to his wishes.(*Garuda Purana*, 95; Dutt, 270)

Thus the ideal Hindu woman is one who sees her highest good in her husband, is devoted to him with a religious zeal and is good and chaste. In other words, she is under the control of her husband, and the wifely role is one of subordination and devotion whatever may be the circumstances. The woman's place is primarily confined to the home, her role limited to procreation and upbringing of children and catering to the needs of her husband. Chastity and control of sexuality are the most important aspects of the role of a wife. The maintenance of chastity requires control of sexuality and a woman's sexuality should always be under the control of man. Before marriage it is the father who controls her, and after marriage it is the husband. In religious literature woman thus controlled is deified and worshipped. A woman as a mother is a subject of much deification and veneration. She is supposed to be a thousand times more vulnerable than the father. From the analysis of Hindu scriptures and other ancient literature it can be concluded that though in the mythological formulations a woman is considered to be physically, spiritually and morally equal to man, in actual social life her expected role is one of subordination to man, perhaps an honourable subordination.

CHAPTER II

Hinduism and its Impact on Women

K.V.K. THAMPURAN*

This short chapter on ' Hinduism and its impact on women' is an attempt at understanding the role Hindu religion has played in moulding the life and outlook of Indian women. Since this is in no way an exhaustive study on the subject, the main objective of the paper is only to provoke investigations on these lines. And for this purpose, we will try to study the popular Hindu scriptures from the following three points of view:-

1. How the Hindu religion was able to influence the life of the men and women of India.

2. The concept of women as contained in the holy books of the Hindus.

3. The role and status of women as indicated in the Hindu scriptures.

At the outset one must understand that unlike the semitic religion, Hinduism is not a static system of philosophical thoughts and religious practices. Hindu religious thoughts and practices have changed/modified themselves during Hinduism's long history of about 5,000 years. During this period it became weak a number of times and almost lost its hold on the people of India but, at the same time, it never failed to get revitalised and return to play a vital role in the life of Hindus. During these vitalisation processes, the introduction of new ideas as well as changes in the interpretation of old ideas took place, creating many sub-divisions out of the old religion. So, any study of the Hindu religion or research based on it, must take into consideration the fact that Hindu society was a conglomeration of Hindu sub-groups following different forms of the same religion. It must also be noted that the Hinduism of the Vedic period was different from that of the Puranic era and again, both these were different in form from that of the

* Mr Thampuran is a member of the Chinmaya Mission., Bangalore

post-Shankara period, even though the contents of all three versions were mainly the same. Consequently, it is very difficult to make generalised statements regarding the influence of Hinduism on the Hindus of India as a whole. Values, customs and traditions varied from place to place and from time to time among the followers of the different groups of Hindus, and therefore allowance must be made before one can come to generalised conclusions regarding the life and way of living of the Hindus of India.

The Reason and Nature of Hindu Influence

Hinduism, like all religions with a long history, for example Christianity, Islam, etc., has played a dominant role in moulding the life of men and women of India. However, it should be noted that though the Hindu religion has had a powerful influence on the life of the people, this influence was not the result of the exercise of formal authority through social, political or economic institutions. Hinduism never exerted the kind of authority which Christianity or Islam could exert on the people because (a) it never had a corporate structure and (b) it had very little association with matters or powers of the State.

Generally speaking, the authority of any religion comes from two sources — from the power and influence of its thoughts and the power and influence of its institutions. In the case of Hinduism, its authority over the followers was mainly due to the power its thoughts had on them.

In order to understand the 'power' religious teachings had on people, their attitudes, behaviour and conduct, we must understand what they were conveying to the listener or the reader. In this connection, it must be understood that the basic purpose behind all religious teachings, and the common quest of all religious masters were all concerning the *quality of life* of man and how to improve the same. It was because the religious masters pointed out how man could improve the quality of human existence that they were listened to, obeyed and even worshipped by the people. All religions tell their followers how they should organise their life and relationships—both private and public—in order to achieve the quality of life pointed out by them.

All religions give reasons for the miseries experienced by man in his life and how to eliminate them. In fact, the difference between the various religions are mainly because of the differences in ideas regarding what causes misery and the methods and means suggested by them for the removal of human suffering. We find in Hinduism the theory of Karma and Re-birth has been the main concept that produced such a profound influence on its followers. We can even say in a general manner that all the different forms of Hindu thought and practices are based on this idea and its interpretations by different Masters at different times.

All religions have their models of the ideal man, ideal woman, ideal family, ideal society, ideal life, etc., through which it influences the attitudes, behaviour and conduct as well as the personality and character of their followers. The religious teachings of the Hindus, its philosophy and mythology, have a large quota of such ideal models which continue to influence the personality, character and way of living of the Hindus. It would not be very wrong to say that even today the heroes of the Hindus are Rama and Sita, Radha and Krishna, etc., and that they try to model their personalities and behaviour on their mythological gods and heroes.

The Hindu View of Women

In order to get an idea of the image of women projected by Hinduism one has to study what the Hindu scriptures have to say about the personality, potential and character of women. That the ancient Hindu religious masters had a fairly good idea about the biological aspects of men, women and the process of human reproduction, etc., is clear from what is written about the same in the *Upanishads* like the *Garbhopanishad, Chandogya Upnishad,* and others.

According to the Hindu scriptures like *Manu Smriti* the male and the female of the human species represent the two halves of the Creator himself. Thus the *Manu Smriti* says :

> Brahma divided himself into two, became man with one half and woman with the other.....(Manu I, 32)

The idea that Man and Woman are the two halves of God the Creator is clearly brought out in the representation of Lord Shiva as the *Ardha Nareeshwara.*

It should also be noted that the Hindu concept of God includes the female as well as the male sex. There are plenty of goddesses in the Hindu religion who are presented as being in no way inferior to the male gods in their potential and capabilities. In this connection it is interesting to note that two things that most men need to improve in their lives—wealth and knowledge—are symbolised by Goddesses Lakshmi and Saraswati respectively in the Hindu Puranas.

To certain groups and branches of Hinduism, the Goddess is the Supreme Creator —the *Shakti*. All the Tantras glorify the feminine as the supreme. In fact it is even mentioned that God Shiva becomes powerful only when joined with Goddess Shakti—*Shiva Shaktyayukta bhavati Shaktah*—the idea being that man is incomplete in his potential until he is associated with woman.

Thus, on the whole, we may say that from the religious point of view of the Hindu scriptures both the male and the female of the species are of equal importance, value and worth and demand the same respect and reverence.

Personality of Women

In the Hindu religion human nature (personality and behaviour) was not studied on a sexist or biological basis. It was believed that human nature and behaviour were basically conditioned and controlled by the *Gunas*, and personality development took place according to the *Dharmas* and *Samskaras* one had adopted. Accordingly they classified all humanity into the four *Varnas*—the Brahmanas, Kshatraiyas, Vaishyas and Shudras, depending on the composition of three *Gunas* of *Saltwa, Rajas* and *Tamas* in the individual, irrespective of whether they were men or women. The famous *Bhagawadgita* says *Chatur varnam maya srishtam guna karma vibhagayo*. It is also said that the compositions of Gunas do change and can be changed by appropriate practices in life.

Potentials of Women

Hindu scriptures viewed women neither as inferior nor superior to men in their potentials and capabilities. Instances are many to indicate that women had developed potentials and skills in many fields in those days. Thus the Upanishads mention many names of exceptionally learned women like Gargi, Maitreyi, etc.—*Maitreyi Brahmavadini Bhabhura*, says the *Brihad-aranyaka* Upanishad. It is mentioned that Subaala gave some very wholesome advice to King Janaka himself. Mention has been also made that women have excelled in the field of men's activities like chariot-driving. Thus, when Arjuna took away Subhadra from the marriage pandal in a chariot, it is mentioned that she told Arjuna that she had also learned to drive a chariot well and would like to enjoy the thrill of driving one through the crowded streets.

Character of Women

There is nothing much in the Hindu scriptures to suggest that women are in any way different from men in character. Women, like men, have been painted as having both the noblest and the meanest of characters at different places. Thus the sage Yagnavalkya considers women as being always pure, as Soma gave them purification, the Gandharva sweet speech and Agni the perfect purity (*Yagnavalkya Smriti*, I-71). At the same time Manu observes that 'women are impure in their desires, wrath, dishonesty, malice and bad conduct'. Even so, Manu and others had a good understanding of the development of human personality and character and regarded them as being influenced by the individual and his/her circumstances. Indicating some of the causes for the distortion of women's character Manu says:

> The taste of intoxicating liquor, the company of the evil, long separation from the husband, much gadding about, excess of sleeping or lying in bed, day-dreaming and constant visits to others' houses and staying there for long periods—these lead to the ruin of women.*(Manu Smriti, V, 148)*

Status of Women as Indicated in Hindu Scriptures

In order to evaluate the status of a member, or group or a class of people one must have a fairly good idea about the amount of power, privileges and share of wealth they have in the organisation to which they belong. To come to conclusions regarding the status of women based on the statements contained in the holy books of the Hindus, it is necessary to understand the Hindu view of life, its meaning and purpose, and the social order that is indicated therein.

According to Hinduism, the quality of human life can be improved only through the attainment of the four *Purushartas* (goals and means of life). These are (1) *Dharma* or duties and responsibilities, (2) *Arta* or wealth, (3) *Kama* or enjoyment and (4) *Moksha* or freedom from the cycle of births and deaths. And, in order to attain these four *Purushartas*, both individually and collectively the Hindu social order of the *Varnashrama* was established with well defined objectives, roles, functions, duties, responsibilities and tasks assigned to the members of each of the four *Varnas* and *Ashramas* as indicated in the diagram given below.

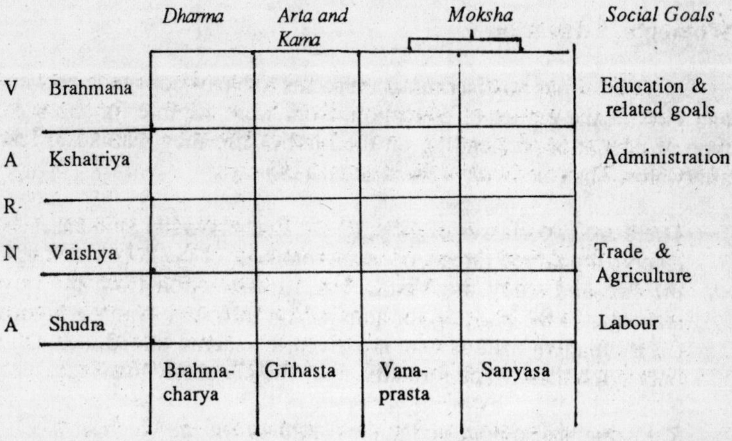

Ashrama

From the above diagram it will be clear that the status of any member in the Hindu society is based on the position he held in the V-A social structure and hierarchy. Rights and privileges were all given to individuals, men, women and children, on the basis of the V-A system of hierarchy. Naturally therefore the status of woman also varied according to to the position she held in the hierarchy at any given time.

It should be noted here that the power, privileges in society given to both the men and women of a particular *Varna* or *Ashrama* were almost similar. The do's and don'ts prescribed (*Acharam* and *Sheelam*) for a particular *Varna* or *Ashrama* were applicable to both men and women more or less equally. However, within the different *Varnas*, the treatment received by women varied considerably. This may be due to the fact that the different *Varnas* had adopted different gods as their favourites and consequently there emerged the value system and the style associated with those particular gods.

The next point that we should consider about the status of ancient Hindu women is how they were treated in comparison to men in those days.

Women's Education

In Vedic times no discrimination seems to have been made between and girls in the matter of education. Both were eligible for the same type of education, depending on the kind of life they wanted to lead afterwards. Thus the *Grahya Sutra* (stanza 24) says:

> There are two classes of girls; (i) the Brahmavadini students, who receive the sacred thread, constant reminder of the holy vows, tend the fire and study the Vedas, but, in distinction from the boy-students, do the begging for alms within their own parental homes, (ii) the Sadyo-Vadhus who are given the sacred thread, somehow only symbolically and formally, immediately before marriage.

The same is also indicated in the *Gautama Smriti*, which says:

> In the olden times, girls also used to wear the sacred thread on the shoulder and the munja-grass string round the waist, and to study the Vedas and recite the *Gayatri.*

Women's Right to Sacraments

There was not much difference between the the kind of sacraments received by Hindu boys and girls of olden India. Thus Manu says:

> All the sacraments prescribed for the boys are prescribed for the girls also. But they are be performed without *veda-mantras*. The marriage sacrament however, obviously, for the bride and grooms alike, has to be performed with *veda-mantras*. (*Manu Smriti* ii-66.)

Women's Status In The House

According to Hindu religious thought, great emphasis is placed on the role of the *Grihasta* or householder. Regarding the status of the householder Manu says:

> Because he nourishes and supports the other *Ashramas* with food for the body and the mind, therefore the householder is the eldest . (*Manu Smriti*, iii-78)

According to the *Upanishad* (*Taithriya Upanishad)* both the father and mother are to be considered as gods—*Matru devo Bhauah* :

According to *Manu Smriti*, the duties of the home must be performed by the husband and wife as a team, (ix-102).

The kind of roles that a Hindu woman played in her husband's life in olden times seems to be no different from what she does today. Thus in the *Ramayana*, Dasharatha says to Kausalya :

> So wife, friend, servant, and as a sister too, also as mother has she been to me. (*Ramayana*, *Aranya*, Ch. 12.)

Women and Marriage

Many forms of marriages were considered socially and religiously acceptable by the Hindu scriptures. In the *Swayamvara* and the *Gandharva* forms of marriage (that is, love marriage) the women had the right to choose her husband. While *inter-varna* marriage was allowed it was prescribed that women should not marry men belonging to a lower *varna* than their own (the *Batiloma* marriage). Indications are also there that during the Vedic period, widows were permitted to marry the younger brother of the dead husband (*Rigveda*, x-18,8).

The practice of polygamy and polyandry were, even though not the accepted norms, not uncommon, and were not looked down upon. Many of the gods and heroes of Hindu mythology had more than one wife. The famous Panda brothers (five brothers) shared a common wife, Draupathi, and yet she has been presented in the *Mahabharata* as a chaste and virtuous woman. What was considered as unrighteous or as sin was unfaithfulness of married partners especially in matters of sex. Extra-marital affairs were considered to be sin, leading to sufferings for the person in this life as well as in the next.

Women's Roles Outside The Home

From what has been said in the *Vedas* and *Puranas* one can draw the conclusion that woman had, in those days, a definite role and function, not only in the home, but outside it also. She had a definite part to play in the *yogas* and *yagnas* and other religious ceremonies conducted by the kings as well as the public. We can also find it mentioned that women, in those days, were employed as governesses and companions to the girls of aristocratic and rich families and as entertainers in the palaces of kings and in temples, and also as secret agents in the employ of the state. Mention has also been made that women who were not economically well-off used to engage in profitable self-employment, doing petty trade, like making and selling cosmetics, food items and so on, to support themselves and their families. It must be remembered that India being an agricultural country, the job opportunities, even for men, in those days, outside the home or the field, were poor.

The Attitude of Men Towards Women

From what we find written in the holy books of the Hindus, it can be seen that during the Vedic period men used to regard women as partners in life as the term *Saha Dharmini* indicates. She was a partner in managing the affairs during the *Grihasta, Vanaprasta* and *Sanyasa Ashrams* in life and consequently must have enjoyed a quality of life comparable to that of the men. But, with the advent of the Puranic era things began to change for the worse as far as the women were concerned.

One of the main reasons for the gradual enhancement in the status of men and a consequent decline in that of the Hindu women, was the change in the earlier religious belief that one can redeem oneself from one's sins only through one's own efforts, to that of the *puranas* which says that by the performance of the *Sraaddha* ceremony by one's own son one can get rid of one's sins even after one's death. This belief naturally increased the value and worth of the sons to the parents, and consequently there was a decline in the status and privileges enjoyed by Hindu women.

Again, with the advent of Buddhism and the emphasis on the monastic life as the means of liberation from the miseries of life, the life of the ascetic was glorified by the people of India. Probably, this influenced the Hindu philosophers and religious leaders who lived after the Buddha, to project the *Grihastå Ashrama* or family life as an obstacle to man's spiritual evolution and salvation. This belief must have made the Hindu men of learning consider women and marriage as bondages in life, and consequently regard and project them as evil, though having some uses. This attitude towards women can be seen even today, among the so-called religious-minded Hindu men.

Conclusion

Any person who wants to study philosophical and religious literature and evaluate it must enquire about the reasons and purposes with which it was written. As far as Hinduism is concerned, it is very clear that the objectives were the development of the human personality, potentials and resources as well socio-political order (the *Dharma Samaj*) necessary for improving the quality of life.*Dukkha Nivruthi* and *Sukha Prapti* are its openly proclaimed goals. It can also be seen that the methods and means recommended for this have all been the outcome of human enquiry and debate and not the injunctions of the gods revealed to a chosen few and held as unalterable for all times to come. The doors of Hindu religion and culture are not closed, and the Hindu women can bring about the changes needed to improve the quality of their lives today as well as for their future growth and development.

CHAPTER III

Women Under the Authority of Islam

ASGHAR ALI ENGINEER*

Religion and rituals are rooted in the social structures from which they arise. No religion can be an exception to this rule, not even revealed religions. The Holy Quran itself proclaims this reality. 'For each (community) we have appointed a divine law and a way of life. Had Allah willed He would have made you one community. He may try you by that which he has given you. so vie one with another in good works.'[1]

It is very clear from the text of the above verse from the holy book that Allah has graced different peoples with different ways and rituals according to which they have to shape their religious and secular lives. Allah did not intend to appoint one uniform law for every people, past and present. Had He intended it, He could have made only one community but He chose otherwise and appointed different ways for different peoples at different times. It is from such verses that Maulana Abdul Kalam Azad derived his revolutionary doctrine of *wahdat-e-adyan* (oneness of essence of religion) and differing shari' as, that is, different laws for different peoples, in keeping with the requirements of socio-temporal realities.[2]

There is a very important thing hinted at in the verse quoted above. Allah did not make one religious community but several and gave each one of them a different way of life in keeping with their genius and temporal requirements so that He might test them. Test in what respect? The answer is to test them as to how best they can shape their lives in order to ensure a better way of life and compete with each other in good deeds in establishing peace and justice.

Thus we see that the Quran takes a sociological view of religion

---

*Asghar Ali Engineer is co-ordinator of the Institute of Islamic Studies.

1 The Quran 5:48.

2 See Commentary on this verse by Maulana Abdul Kalam Azad in his Tarjuman al-Quran Vol. II, pp. 632-33.

and rituals which comes very close to the modern scientific approach. And this is precisely the point in approaching the question of women, like other questions, in the Islamic context. The normative side of religion finds its sociological interpretation in keeping with the social structure. We will elaborate this a little later. What is important is to emphasise the sociological approach.

Social dynamics bring about a dialectical interaction between the empirical and the ideological. The normative legal structure of a people must be examined in the light of this interaction. When the social structure is sought to be changed in the light of an ideology (revealed or otherwise) empirical realities assert themselves. Finally what emerges is both contextual (empirical) and normative (ideological). The Islamic shari'a also is a synthesis of contextual and normative elements. The Islamic legalists as well as historians have thrown detailed light on pre-Islamic practices some of which influenced the later Islamic practices.

7

I.Pre-Islamic and Later Islamic Practices

The pre-Islamic social structure was tribal and is referred to as *jahilliyah* (that is, a period of ignorance) in Islamic literature. The Quranic revelations provided people with the knowledge to combat *jahilliyah* practices. Tribal society has no written or revealed laws, only customs and usages; as had the pre-Islamic Arab society. The customs and usages, sanctified by age-old practices were followed irrespective of whether they were unjust or oppressive to certain sections of society. The only argument in their favour was that they found their forefathers following these practices. They argued with the prophets, 'How can we forsake what we found our forefathers upon' ? They said: 'Hast thou come unto us that we should serve Allah alone and forsake what our father worshipped ?'[3]

Here we are mainly concerned with the status of women. In pre-Islamic society the position of women was considerably lower. The tribes were patriarchal in structure and generally assigned to women a much lower social status. The widows of fathers were inherited. The Quran refers to this practice and prohibits it. 'And marry not those women whom your fathers married, except what hath already happened (of that nature) in the past. Lo! It was ever lewdness and abomination,

7

3 The Quran 7:70, See also 11:62, 14:10, 16:35 etc.

and an evil way'.[4]

There were many abominable customs and usages in respect of women in the period of ignorance. Despite a measure of freedom, the overall status of women was much inferior in pre-Islamic society. If Islamic laws, the source of which is mainly divine revelations and their exemplification through the prophetic practices (*sunna*), are seen in the context of *jahilliyyah* practices, they will appear to be no less than revolutionary. The Quran greatly improved the social status of women and laid down definite norms, as against mere customs and usages. They could no longer be treated as mere chattels to be traded or objects of sexual lust. The married women thus were described by the Quran as *muhsanat*, meaning chaste and secured.

During the period of ignorance there were no norms and laws as far as divorce and marriage on the one hand, and inheritance and property rights of women on the other, were concerned. One could marry as many women as one liked, could divorce them any time without any obligation as to maintenance, could even enter into temporary marriage contracts (*muta'as* marriage) and similar other practices.[5] There were no definite norms and laws.

The Quran, however, not only did away with all arbitrary practices but set out definite norms and gave women a definite status though not strictly equal to that of man. But the status accorded was very nearly equal to man's and seen in the then prevailing social context, it was definitely a revolutionary step. The Quran declares in unambiguous terms, 'And they (women) have rights similar to those (of men) over them in kindness, and men are a degree above them. Allah is Mighty, Wise.'[6]

The above verse must be carefully analysed and understood. The Quran makes it clear that women have rights similar to those of men, yet further on, it says that men are a degree above them. The two statements might appear to be contradictory but seen in the proper context, one would see that this contradictoriness reflects a social reality and that given the social reality the contradictoriness could not be easily resolved in favour of women. Also the words 'Allah is Mighty, Wise' are quite significant. Allah is Mighty enough to accord equal status to

---

4 The Quran 4: 22.

5 For pre-Islamic customs about marriage, divorce etc. see Kinship and Marriage

6 The Quran 2:228.

women but wisdom lay in recognising certain social realities and acting accordingly. Mere mightiness might upset the social balance, thus causing more complex problems. Though Allah's intention is to accord equal status to women, the social context does not admit of it right away, and in His wisdom, He allows men slight superiority over women.

In yet another verse, the reason for this degree of superiority is stated clearly. 'Men are in charge of women because Allah hath made the one of them to excel the other, and because they spend of their property (for the support of women), so good women are obedient (to Allah), guarding in the secret that which Allah had guarded.'[7]

In the then Arabian society women were not expected or required to earn and look after the family. This was exclusively man's obligation and preserve. It could not have been otherwise in the then sociological context. Since he was charged with the obligation of looking after the sustenance of the family he was also accorded a degree of superiority over woman. It was so in Allah's wisdom. Since Allah's wisdom cannot be arbitrary, if the social context changes and if women also begin to earn (and there is nothing in the holy book or in the prophetic *sunna* preventing women from earning their livelihood or that of the family) and look after the family, there will be nothing to prevent them from acquiring either equal status or even a degree of superiority over men. The Quran has certainly not shied away, as shown by the earlier verse (2:228), from pronouncing the doctrine of equality of sexes.

In any society in transition, whatever the ideological perspective for the future social set-up, one cannot completely snap the relationship with the past. We have already referred to dialectical interaction between the empirical and ideological in determining the resultant reality which ultimately prevails. The Divine Wisdom cannot ignore the empirical. It is again in this spirit that Allah makes it very clear that each (community) has its own appointed law and way of life. It is an empirical reality that one should not quarrel; instead vie with each other to do good. Empirical reality does assert itself even if the ideologues might wish otherwise.

While referring to empirical reality one has to bear in mind that while the ideological is transcendent, empirical reality is subject to change in a changing society. The theologians, however, either

---

[7] The Quran 4:35

completely ignore empirical reality or do not take changes in it into account. Moreover, and this is worse, they often confuse the compound of ideological and static empirical reality as unchangeable, transcendental theology. The Quranic theology, on the other hand, is neither dogmatic nor ignorant of empirical reality which tends to be dynamic. The great Islamic thinkers like Muhammad Abduh, Syed Ahmad Khan, Iqbal and others realised this.

Some of the pre-Islamic customs in form, if not in content, as an empirical reality, did intrude upon later Islamic practices. The *sunna*—both the words and deeds of the Prophet—had many elements of these pre-Islamic customs. These were unique to the Arabs of the region.

However, the Quranic revelations were not only contextual but also normative and hence have transcendental validity. But one has to carefully sort out contextual from normative both in the Quran as well as in *sunna*. The whole *juris corpus* of Islam has to be examined in this light.

The necessity of changes is acutely felt with the movement in the social base. Conservatism, while necessary to an extent to ensure continuity of what is best and most healthy in the past, cannot stand up to the pressures for genuine change. Moreover, it kills what is the creative best in human beings. Change in the social base demands creative response from human beings in order to make life more meaningful and worthwhile. The acclaimed poet, Iqbal, observes :

> The ultimate spiritual basis of all life, as conceived by Islam, is eternal and reveals itself in variety and change. A society based on such a conception of Reality must reconcile, in its life, the categories of permanence and change. It must possess eternal principles to regulate its collective life, for the eternal gives us a foothold in the world of perpetual change. But eternal principles when they are understood to exclude all possibilities of change which, according to the Quran, is one of the greatest 'signs' of God, tend to immobilise what is essentially mobile in its nature.[8]

He then more categorically states a need for change in the legal principles of Islam in the light of modern experience:

---

[8] Dr. Sir Muhammed Iqbal, *The Reconstruction of Religious Thought in Islam*, Lahore, 1960, pp.147-48.

> The claim of the present generation of Muslim liberals to reinterpret the foundational legal principles, in the light of their own experience and the altered conditions of modern life is, in my opinion, perfectly justified. The teaching of the Quran that life is a process of progressive creation necessitates that each generation, guided but unhampered by the work of its predecessors, should be permitted to solve its own problems.[9]

But unfortunately conservatism is too dominant in the world of Islam to permit any change. The theologians have usurped the right of the modern generation of Muslims to avail themselves of their own experience to reconstruct creatively what is eternal in the religio-legal inheritance. Iqbal's voice of sanity has religated to an obscure corner while his poetry, rich in Islamic emotions and representing the aspirations of the Muslim elite, is highly acclaimed.

However, there is a genuine problem which sociologists of religion must grapple with. Conservatism, though a mental attitude, also has a social base. Conservatism finds a deeper anchor firstly in an unchanging society and secondly, though it appears strange and rather contradictory it is nevertheless true, in a rapidly changing society. In the second category of society conservatism provides an inner defence-mechanism to deal with an 'externally perceived threat' and that is how change is perceived by those who do not benefit from it. There is one more factor to be taken into account which is responsible for building up resistance to change.

Many of the Islamic countries are embroiled in an anti-imperialist struggle. They consider the imperialism of the West a threat to their religion and culture. The ideology of modernisation is thus supplanted by the ideology of anti-imperialism. Modernisation is perceived as closer to, or the same as, westernisation and opposed. This phenomenon can be clearly witnessed today in Iran. The Shah of Iran symbolised American imperialism and he initiated a programme of modernisation benefitting the upper classes. Ali Shari'ati and others highly effectively used Islam as an ideology to oppose both the political and cultural onslaught of western imperialism.[10] Any change was perceived as an

---

[9] *Op.cit.*, pp. 168

[10] Ali Shari'ati, a highly articulate western trained sociologist, interpreted Islam so as to effectively oppose the repressive policies of the Shah. He made religion highly respectable and gave it a radical thrust. He used to draw huge audiences in Iran and the cassettes of his speeches sold by thousands. The Shah's

onslaught and opposed.

Also, in other countries the Islamic opposition labels the ruling elite as collaborators with imperialism and generates pressures for establishing an Islamic State. The ruling elites, in response to these pressures, project themselves as more conservative than their opponents and introduce ' Islamic measures'. One has to keep all this in mind while trying to analyse the phenomenon of neo-conservatism or the wave of fundamentalism in the Islamic World.

The status of woman also becomes an integral part of such political processes. Her status becomes as much a symbol of political struggle as anything else. The authors of *In the Shadow of Islam* inform us :

.. in three historical moments *chador* (the veil) was turned into a symbol. At the time of Reza Shah's compulsory unveiling, for a woman to appear without it symbolised modernity and change; during the Revolution of 1979, wearing it symbolised resistance to the Shah ; and finally, at the time of the construction of the Islamic Republic, its imposition symbolised progress for the Islamic side and regression for others. At other times wearing or not wearing the *chador* was a matter of personal choice, [12] whether for reasons of religion or poverty, habit, convenience and so on. It did not imply taking sides, whether ideologically or politically.[11]

In India too, the question of any change in Muslim personal law is primarily political and can hardly be decided on its merits, religious or otherwise. Religion is subject to various interpretations and in today's complex situation the predominant interpretation is often determined by political rather than purely religious considerations. About Iran we are told, 'The question of Islam versus women's emancipation did not fully arise until later, when the power struggle of Reza Shah against the clergy made it a question, and again when the Shah's white revolution brought Islam versus Westernism and nationalism (in general and as regards to the women's situation) into head-on collision.[12]

The case of Indian Muslims is no less complex. Sociologically

---

agents murdered him in London.

12

[11] Azar Tapari and Hahid Yeganah, *In the Shadow of Islam*—The Women's Movement in Iran, London, 1982, pp. 31.

[12] *Ibid.*

they are quite backward, both socially and economically. The rural population (around 72% in the case of Muslims) does not matter much in the debate for reforms. It is the urban population which plays an important role in such matters. The urban population as far as Muslims are concerned is predominantly of artisans. Artisans are generally socially backward and religiously conservative, especially when industrialisation is taking place and many of them are getting uprooted, as it means a threat to their economic security. Others among the urban Muslims are petty traders, doers of odd jobs and workers. The professional middle-class, modern in outlook and one which feels most for change and reform, is very weak. It is unable to exert sufficient pressure for change and in the face of its weakness tends to be conservative.

Such an atmosphere can hardly be congenial for the needed change. Religious change, or change in any traditional society arouses stiff opposition. It requires, in order to be successful, not only a felt need in a large section of society, but also a dedicated group of committed reformers. Also, the community among which reforms are being advocated must be fully secure and confident of itself. There should not be any perceived or real threats to its security. Communal riots and strong communal propaganda on the part of communalists often create difficulties for those who advocate reform.

Often the demand for reforms in the personal law emanates from communal quarters, thus rightly creating the impression that it is a stick to beat Muslims with rather than a genuine desire to improve the status of Muslim women. There are undoubtedly genuine elements among those who advocate change but they are outnumbered and often misunderstood. In such a complex situation the religious merit of reforms hardly matters. It is the minority perception, the political role of its leadership and the near absence of a strong desire for change in keeping with the true spirit of religion that finally decide the outcome. In such a situation impatience will not help. The reformers and advocates of change should not only have a great reserve of patience but should also have the right perception of the situation and proper assessment of various factors inhibiting change in order to chalk out the proper course.

II.The Veil and Polygamy: The Social Context

The way certain laws are practised by Muslims has created a lot of misunderstanding about them. It is wrong to maintain, as some less knowledgeable Muslims do, that the Shari'a is wholly divine. It is certainly based on the Holy Quran and *sunna* and to that extent it certainly carries elements of divinity in it. But there is also an element of human opinion (the opinion of great Imams who compiled and codified the laws into what is now known as Shari'a *ra'i, qiyas* (analogy) and *ijtihad* (exertion to properly interpret in keeping with the situation). These thinkers and compilers of *Shari'a* were certainly influenced by their own milieu which was predominantly male-dominated. No human being can escape such influences.

The Prophet was extremely kind to women but the constraint of the male-dominated environment influenced his decisions also. One anecdote in this respect is quite interesting. 'It is related' says Prof. S.T. Lokhandwala, that on one occasion the Prophet said : "Beat not your wives ". Then Umar came to the prophet and said: 'Our wives will get an upper hand over their husbands from hearing this'. He also claimed that the Quraish (the tribe of the Prophet) always ruled their women and the Ansars (the people of Medinah) were always ruled by their women . So the Prophet agreed to keep the Arab social custom unchanged. Then a large number of women collected round the prophet's family, and complained of their husbands' beating them. So the Prophet said, 'Verily a great number of women are gathered here in my house complaining of their husbands and those men who beat their wives do not behave well. He is not of my way who teaches a woman to go astray'.[13]

The above incident clearly shows the social pulls and pressures the Prophet, the great lawgiver, had to work under. He could not have ignored certain social realities of his time. The contextual factor, as far as *Hadith* and Prophetic practices are concerned, will have to be taken into account before drawing any conclusion. No law can totally free itself from the social context. Divine wisdom also lay in not ignoring the social context. Most of the revealed verses in the Quran pertaining to socio-economic or legal matters are called *mu'amalat* — social context. This context must be carefully evaluated in order to correctly understand the import of any such verse.

As far as women are concerned this can be illustrated by taking the

---

[13] See Mishkat Babu-n-Nikah, quoted by Prof. S.T. Lokhandwala, 'The Position of Women under Islam ' in *Islamic Perspective*, Vol.I, January 1984, ed. by Asghar Ali Engineer.

questions of the veil and polygamy, both highly controversial issues in our social context. First let us take the question of the veil. The verse quoted in support of the veil is as follows : ' O Prophet ! Tell thy wives and thy daughters and the women of the believers to draw their cloaks close round them (*udnina*) (when they go abroad). That will be better, so that they may not be recognised and not annoyed.'[14]

Firstly, in this verse the context is clear from the portion underlined. There were hypocrites and anti-social elements who used to tease. Muslim women and when caught and reprimanded would maintain that they did not know that they (that is the Muslim women) were Muslims.In order that the Muslim women be recognised, they were instructed to draw their cloak closer to the face. The main intention of this verse, according to Zamakhshari, the great M'utazalite commentator of the Quran, is to distinguish *hurrah* (free woman) from *amat* (slave woman) so that free woman is recognised and not harassed or teased.[15] Zamakshari maintains that the emphasis is on being recognised. Thus the real intention of drawing the cloak closer is to be recognised as a free woman. The context of the verse is thus very clear. First there is no mention of veiling the face and secondly it is not an obligatory order for all time to come. If the context changes, the reason adduced disappears; it would no longer be binding.

Another important verse in this respect is from chapter 24. It says:

> And say to the believing women that they should lower their gaze and guard their modesty; that they should not display their beauty and ornaments except what (must ordinarily) appear thereof, that they should draw their veils over their bosom and not display their beauty except to their husbands, their fathers.. and that they should not strike their feet in order to draw attention to their hidden ornaments.[16]

Here also there is no mention of veiling of the face. The whole emphasis is on modesty and avoidance of unnecessary beauty and adornment in order to attract man's attention. To use the modern feminist movement's jargon, women should not be made an object of lust. Her way of dressing should be such as to protect her individuality and dignity as a woman. Imam Fakhr al-Din Razi, another celebrated

---

14 The Quran 33.

15 See Zamakhshari Al-Kashshaf, Vol. III, Beirut, pp. 274.

16 The Quran 24:31.

commentator of the Quran, also maintains that there is no veiling of face required as hands and face remain exposed by way of natural habit.[17] It is interesting to note that the Quran admonishes men also to be modest and keep their gaze lowered. 'Say to the believing to note that they should lower their gaze and guard their modesty; that will make for greater purity for them.'[18] This verse precedes the one admonishing women to be modest. Thus the Quran requires of both men and women to be modest. It was only male domination which put women under the veil and confinement without corresponding rigorous sexual behaviour on the men's part.

The case of polygamy is not much different. What was permitted in a certain social context and with great reluctance was taken by men as licence to marry up to four women. This is far from the Quranic spirit and social context. Polygamy has been permitted by the Quran in a concrete social context and in order to do justice to the weak (that is, orphans) and subject to the condition that equality of treatment would be ensured and the Quran itself makes it very clear that equality of treatment is almost an impossible condition to meet.

As for ploygamy the Quran says:

> They ask you concerning women, say Allah gives you decree concerning them and the Scripture which has been recited unto you (gives decree) about orphan women to whom you do not give back what is due to them (namely their properties which are under your charge) but you would rather marry them, and also (concerning) the weak among children, and that you should deal justly with orphans. You will never be able to deal equally between (your) wives, however much you wish (to do so), so do not incline away completely from one, leaving her suspended.[19]

The other verse on polygamy is worded thus:

> Give unto orphans their wealth and do not exchange (their) good properties with your bad ones, nor consume their properties by mixing them with yours; it is indeed a great sin. But if you cannot do justice to orphans, then you marry from among (orphan ?)

---

[17] See Maulanna Muhammad Ali's *Bayan al-Quran*, Vol. II, (Lahore, 1388 A.H.), pp. 964.

[18] The Quran 24:30.

[19] *Ibid.*, 4:127-129.

women such as please you—two, three or four. If, however, you fear you cannot do justice (among cowives) then marry only one or (marry) women-slaves, this would be nearest to avoiding injustice.[20]

It is very clear from the wordings of these verses on polygamy that both have been revealed in the context of orphan girls and the primary concern is justice both with the properties of orphans and cowives, if their wards marry more than one. There was the problem of justice with orphans, and in pre-Islamic society the Arabs used to take any number of wives. The orphans were weak and subject to injustices in respect of their properties at the hands of their guardians. In order to ensure justice to the orphans Allah permitted their guardians to marry either from amongst these orphans or their mothers up to four so that they and their properties would be looked after properly. The number of wives was restricted to four, justice was ensured to the orphans and men were strictly warned to do equal justice to all the wives, otherwise to marry only one. Thus we see that justice was the primary concern whether for orphans, for the weak or for the women as wives.

Seen thus in the proper social context the verses on polygamy are not a general permission, let alone an open licence, to take more than one wife. Firstly, it has been permitted only to ensure justice to orphan girls or women. If one does not have any such problem of looking after orphans, the question of taking more than one wife does not arise at all. Secondly, this solution also was suggested in the context of Arabian society where polygamy was quite common, that too with a rider to do equal justice to all the wives, or take only one.

If one keeps this context in mind and also the modern social context, and the increasingly greater social role played by women, their sharpened sense of equality make polygamy as good as banned. Moreover, the Holy Quran's unabating insistence on justice should get precedence over everything. One should also bear in mind that the sense of justice also has a social context. What was considered just in a medieval society may not be considered so in our context today. The Quran, morever, does not negate, as pointed out earlier, the dynamics of social change and context of social justice. Polygeny, polygamy or monogamy may not be perfect models of social justice; it is only the social context which would decide the general acceptance or rejection of a particular mode of marriage. It is wrong to consider any of them as the

---

20 The Quran 4:2:3.

perfect model.

One thing is more than apparent from many verses of the Quran. Normatively speaking, it tends to treat the two sexes as equal on the human plane. This doctrine of equality of sexes has been enunciated in terms of legal rights when it states: 'For them (women) there are rights (against men) that are exactly commensurate with their obligations (towards them)'[21] and in terms of reward in religious merit when it says, ' Lo ! men who surrender unto Allah and women who surrender, and men who believe and women who believe, and men who obey and women who obey, and men who speak the truth and women who speak truth, and men who persevere (in righteousness) and women who persevere, and men who are humble and women who are humble, and men who fast and women who fast, and men who guard their modesty and women who guard (their modesty), and men who remember Allah and women who remember—Allah has prepared for them forgiveness and a vast reward'.[22]

I do not think more equality than this could be promised in any other religious scripture.

Divorce and Mulsim Women

The recent Supreme Court judgement granting maintenance to a Muslim woman after divorce beyond the period of *iddah* (generally three months after the divorce takes effect) has attracted wide attention among those who advocate reform in the law as it operates today, and those who oppose any change ostensibly on the ground that it is divine and hence cannot admit of any change.

The Supreme Court judgement pertains to Shah Banu Begum of Indore who was divorced by her husband, advocate Mohammed Ahmad Khan, in November 1978. They were married in 1932 and have three sons and two daughters: The husband paid her maintenance at the rate of Rs. 200 per month from the time he drove her out in 1975 until he divorced her and including the period of *iddah*, that is, three months after the divorce.

The aggrieved woman filed a suit against her former husband claiming maintenance beyond the period of *iddah* under Section 125

---

21 The Quran 4:228.

22 The Quran 33:36

Cr. PC in the court of the Judicial Magistrate (First Class), at the rate of Rs. 500 per month. She alleged that her husband earned Rs. 60,000 a year. The court granted her a paltry sum of Rs. 25 per month. In a revision application before the Madhya Pradesh High Court the maintenance amount was revised to Rs. 179.20 per month. The husband filed an appeal against this in the Supreme Court.

The Supreme Court upheld the divorcee's contention for maintenance beyond the *iddah* period and applied Section 125 Cr. P.C as the Muslim Personal Law does not admit any maintenance beyond the period of *iddah*. In this case the Supreme Court observed, 'There is no conflict between the provisions of Section 125 Cr. PC and those of the Muslim Personal Law on the question of the Muslim husband's obligation to provide maintenance for a divorced wife who is unable to maintain herself.' For hearing this case a five-judge Constitution Bench headed by Chief Justice Y. V. Chandrachud was constituted.

The Court rejected the husband's contention that the wife is entitled to *mahar* (dower paid by husband for contracting marriage), and no more for maintenance after she is divorced. The Court observed that if *mahar* is the amount which the wife is entitled to receive from the husband in consideration of the marriage, that is the very opposite of the amount being payable in consideration of divorce.

Here we would like to throw some light on this important controversy. The judgement is bound to have far-reaching consequences as far as personal laws of various communities are concerned.The Supreme Court itself was aware of this when it observed. '...inevitably the role of the reformer has to be assumed by the courts because it is beyond the endurance of sensitive minds to allow injustice to be suffered when it is so palpable.'

The judgement is of great interest and importance and will be supported and opposed with great passion. Those who support any change or reform in Muslim Personal Law are : (1) Those who want to fight injustices against the weaker sex and male domination. This category includes many militant women's organisations (who also fight against bride-burning, cruelty against women, etc.), as well as those who genuinely desire change and reform in keeping with the conditions of modern times. (2) The second category includes those who are not genuinely concerned with reform but nevertheless want change in Muslim Personal Law on the grounds that Muslims are enjoying certain undesirable privileges like taking more wives than one and divorcing them at their will while the Hindus are compelled to practise monogamy and cannot divorce their wives unilaterally. In other words, their motives are communal rather than secular or genuine feeling for suffering women.

Among those who oppose any reform or change in Muslim Personal Law there are two categories: First, those who oppose for political reasons in order to promote their own leadership by playing up emotional issues. These theologians and secular leaders from amongst Muslims have made retention of Muslim Personal Law a key issue in Muslim politics at the cost of more relevant secular issues being faced by Muslims. Secondly, there is a large number of Muslims who genuinely think that the *Shari'at* (mainly Hanafite school of jurisprudence followed by the majority of Sunni Muslims in India) is totally divine and hence immutable and there is no place for any reform or change through human agency, whatever the merit of the case for reform. Those who hold this opinion are in overwhelming majority among Indian Muslims today.

When there are powerful vested interests on both sides of the divide (theologians and Muslim politicians who have made it a key issue of Muslim politics, and Hindu communalists who are bent upon forcing change and who give vent to their chauvinistic feelings on this issue), it becomes very difficult to conduct the debate on change in a rational and dispassionate way.

A couple of weeks before the Supreme Court judgement, at a well-attended Muslim Personal Law Board meeting at Calcutta in the first week of April, the Board's President, Maulana Abul Hasan Ali Nadvi, said in a highly emotional tone that Muslim Personal Law was based on the Quran and Sunnah, and renouncing it would amount to renouncing the holy book and Sunnah which means *kufr* (unbelief) and a Muslim under no circumstances would accept *kufr*. This report was carried by *Azad Hind,* an Urdu daily from Calcutta. Similarly, Banatwala of the Indian Union Muslim League, demanded in Parliament, in the first week of April, deletion of Article 44 (pertaining to introduction of a uniform civil code) from the Constitution. Such speeches and events are widely covered by the Urdu press and reinforce the feelings of Muslim masses for no change whatsoever.

The Hindu communalists, on the other hand, carry on vicious propaganda for a uniform civil code on the grounds that most Muslims take four wives and produce innumerable children, thus multiplying their population, and would soon outnumber the Hindus. At the time of the Ekatmata Yagna organised by the Vishwa Hindu Parishad last year, pamphlets were distributed depicting a Muslim man with four wives with the slogan ' We five, ours twenty-five'. It is highly mischievous propaganda which creates strong apprehension in the minds of Hindus about the fast-multiplying population of Muslims and possibility of another Pakistan. Some communalist Hindus have filed a petition in the Calcutta High Court demanding also a ban on the Quran on the plea that it incites Muslims to kill *kafirs*. The petition was filed on April 16, 1985 under Article 226 of the Constitution and Section 95 Cr.PC and Section 153(A) and 295(A) IPC. Fortunately, it was rejected by the Calcutta High Court, but it has to be noted that such moves can only exacerbate communal feeling rather than create a genuine atmosphere for religious reform and change.

Let us examine the case for change or reform in the Muslim Personal Law as it operates today in India. We will particularly deal with the case of maintenance as the Supreme Court judgement pertains to this question. First and foremost it must be borne in mind that the *Shari'ah* as compiled by eminent and revered jurists is not wholly divine. It is undoubtedly based on the Quran and Sunnah but also on *ra'i* (human opinion of those jurists), *ijtihad* (personal exertion and interpretation) and *qiyas* (analogy), and that is why there are many differences between different schools of law. These differences are no doubt mostly on *furu'at* (That is, on matters of detail) but in certain respects are also of a fundamental nature. The Sunnis, for example, consider *mut'a* marriage as forbidden whereas the Shias uphold it. Had the *Shari'at* been wholly divine, no such differences whether of a fundamental nature or in matters of detail would have existed. Thus the *Shari'at* has both components, divine as well as human. It is the latter component which, with the change of circumstances, stands in need of change as the great jurists themselves had used their human judgement for compilation of *Shari'ah* in their own circumstances.

The differences between various jurists can be explained by the differences in their geographical, social, and temporal situations. Imam Hanbal and Imam Malik belonged to Mecca and Medina and hence were closer to the Quranic and Medinese traditions as they did not have to face new problems which arose in far-off places like Baghdad, Basra, Egypt and Damascus where people of diverse origins, different outlooks and multiple traditions mixed together thus throwing up a variety of problems. A variety of problems had begun to arise with the conquests of far-off places and the four rightly guided Caliphs had to confront and tackle many problems. The great jurists who were engaged in the serious enterprise of compiling *Shari"ah* in the second and third century Hijrah (8th and 9th century AD) and in quite far-off places had naturally to face a greater variety of problems which they tried to tackle in the light of the Quran and *Sunnah* using their own opinion.

One can hardly ignore the fact that it was a man-dominated milieu and jurists could not but give more benefits to men while using their opinion on various matters and their details whether pertaining to maintenance, custody of children, different forms of divorce, marital options, guardians' rights, etc. It could not have been otherwise in such a milieu. Equal status of women would not have been accepted by society at large. However, it does not mean that the laws as codified by the great jurists using their opinion and interpretation should be treated as immutable. With changes of circumstances, certain inevitable changes in the components based on *ra'i* (opinion) must be subjected to change.

As for the influence of circumstances, it is interesting to note the case of irrevocable divorce in one sitting. In this form of divorce, the husband can, in one sitting, pronounce the word *talaq* thrice to make it irrevocable divorce. It is *talag al-bid'a* (that is, innovated divorce) which has not been prescribed by the Quran or Sunnah of the Prophet. In fact there are instances in which the Prophet is reported to have frowned upon the practice of pronouncing *talaq* thrice in one sittiing. (See Mishkat Sharif, vol. 1 Bag al-Khul'a was al-Talaq, Delhi, n.d, p. 711) Most theologians are agreed that this form of divorce was introduced by the second Caliph Hazaarat Umar in order to punish some unscrupulous persons who had taken divorce very lightly.

It should also be noted that the prevalent method of *talaq* among the Indian Muslims (mainly Hanafis) is not in keeping with either the Quran or Sunna. According to the prevalent method a Hanafi Muslim can pronounce *talaq* thrice in one sitting and it becomes an irrevocable divorce. Even if the word *talaq* is pronounced thrice in the state of inebriation, anger, or by way of fun, divorce would be valid. It is this form of divorce which has become a cause of great suffering for thousands of Muslim women.

The Quran does not refer to this form of divorce. According to the Quran one can give only one divorce after every menstrual course (called *talaq-i-raj-'i*, that is, revocable divorce) and divorce will become irrevocable if it is repeatedly pronounced thrice over a period of three menstrual courses. Thus there would be enough opportunity for reconciliation if divorce had been pronounced in a state of anger or due to temporary conflict between husband and wife.

Thus the Quran says :

Women who are divorced shall wait, keeping themselves apart, three (monthly) courses. And it is not lawful for them that they should conceal that which Allah hath created in their wombs if they are believers in Allah and the Last Day. *And their husbands would do better to take them back in that case if they desire a reconciliation.* And they (women) have rights similar to those (of men) over them in kindness ... (2:228).

Further the Quran says:'Divorce must be pronounced twice and they (a woman) must be retained in honour or released in kindness' (2:229)

Thus it can be seen that there is no concept of three *talaqs* in one sitting. as practised by the Muslims, in the holy book. In fact this practice was followed by the Arabs during *jahilliyah* (pre-Islamic period) and the Prophet is reported to have expressed his anger on such a form of divorce. The practice came back after the death of the Prophet as it was advantageous to men. It is highly regrettable that the Muslim jurists defend this form of un-Quranic divorce as an integral part of Islam and even consider it divine. There are clear injunctions against this form of divorce both in the Quran and Sunnah. All the eminent theologians accept this.

One must remember that the Quran does not permit indiscriminate divorce. The words of the Quran '(a woman) must be retained in honour and released in kindness' make its intention very clear. The wife must be treated with honour in wedlock (she must retain her individuality and dignity) and released with 'kindness' (that is divorced) if a smooth and dignified life in wedlock is not ensured. Unfortunately all such directives of the Quran have been thrown to the winds by the Muslims.

The Supreme Court judgement is about payment of maintenance to the divorced wife. It is true that all schools of Islamic jurisprudence restrict maintenance to the period of *iddah*, that is, either three months from the time divorce takes effect or, if the wife is pregnant, until she gives birth to her child. The Quran uses very kind words for the divorced wives. The Quranic verse says:

'Lodge them where you dwell, according to your wealth, and harass them not so as to straighten life for them. And if they are with child, then spend for them till they bring forth their burden. Then, if they give such for you, give them due payment and consult together in kindness ...' (Quran 65 :6).

The Quran exhorts men to look after their divorced wives in the same manner as they look after themselves and not to throw them out with a pittance. Though provision for the period of *iddah* has not been clearly mentioned in the verse, its implication is clear from the section of the verse which refers to the bringing forth of a child if the woman is carrying.

However, the social context of the Quranic injunction should also be kept in mind as Allah's injunctions cannot be devoid of social wisdom and social justice for both men and women. In Arabian society, firstly it was no stigma for a woman if she was divorced, secondly she could easily revert to her parents who looked after her until she remarried. In such a social context it was not necessary for her to be provided for beyond the period of *iddah* when she was again free to remarry and in most of the cases she did.

However, the Quran, in order to prevent injustice even in exceptional cases when the woman could not marry or had no one to look after her during the period of *iddah*, also said, 'For divorced women a provision in kindness: a duty for those who ward off (evil).' (Quran 2:241). Though it may not be compulsory for man to provide for his divorced wife beyond the period of *iddah* in normal cases, it may be provided for even beyond *iddah* in kindness and also by way of duty in cases where it might lead to social evil. In any case it is social justice which is more important. It is keeping in view this provision of the Quran that some Muslim countries have provided for maintenance of the divorced wives beyond the period of *iddah*, as for example the Syrian Law of 1953 which has made such a provision on the basis of the above verse. (See Tahir Mahmood, *Family Law Reform in the Muslim World)*.

Syed Shahabuddin, in a letter to the *Indian Express* (May 8, 1985) says, 'Can the Supreme Courte cite a single authority on Muslim law who has permitted maintenance to a divorcee beyond the *iddah* period ? Can the Supreme Court cite any Muslim country where it has been allowed ?' Political compulsions apart, let Shahabuddin study the change introduced in many Muslim countries in *ahwal alshakhisiyah* (personal laws) and he would know the scope of these changes. Syria, as pointed out above, has certainly made such a provision beyond the period of *iddah.* Also, whether or not any other religious authority has, because of his personal opinions or the circumstances in which he lived, thought it fit or not fit to make provision for divorcees beyond the period of *iddah*, Allah has certainly provided for it in deserving cases as is obvious from the Quranic verse (2:241).

It is really unfortunate that for political compulsions even the provisions of the holy book, in matters of divorce and maintenance beyond the period of *iddah* are being overlooked. In circumstances prevailing in India, divorce often becomes a social stigma and the divorcee finds it difficult to remarry and in many cases there is no one to look after her after she has been arbitrarily and unilaterally divorced. The conditions in our country are very diffrent from those of the Middle Eastern society in matters of marriage and divorce. Our social ethos, therefore, requires proper interpretation of the divine junctions. Kindness and obligation to social justice and justice to weaker sections is repeatedly emphasised by the Holy Quran. The combination of 'kindness' and 'obligation' is important to note. If out of kindness one provides for the divorcee beyond of the period of *iddah* in cases where there is no wherewithal for the woman, that is good; but if one does not do so it may have to be made obligatory, to ward off social evils.

If we are honest about doing justice to women in the right spirit of the Quran there is no need to get agitated over the Supreme Court judgement. This judgement should, instead, lead us to introspection about certain uses and misuses of Muslim Personal Law in India in favour of men and to a serious bid at reform. The Quran has hinted at slight male superiority (it was natural in the social circumstances then prevailing) but it has certainly not advocated the concept of male domination. But latter developments unfortunately imposed total male domination in violation of the Quranic spirit. Modern conditions have made male domination all the more repugnant. Shall we take note of divine injunctions overcoming old male prejudices and political compulsions?

CHAPTER IV

Impact of Islam on the Status of Women from the Socio-Cultural Point of View

MUZAMMIL SIDDIQUI,*

In a male-dominated world and among the volatile minority communities in India, especially the Muslims, an open and frank discussion about the comparative status of women is fraught with risks. It is more likely than not to touch off an emotional disturbance, if indeed not an outburst. Both the diction and the tone of the argument, though not necessarily its content, must perforce be kept in a low key.

Humankind is millions of years old. Most of the known religions of the world are, however, of recent origin. In pre-historic times, when man lived in the wilds, the quest for food and perpetuation of the tribe provided the primary, if not the only, motive force. The women, because of their physiological limitations had virtually no role to play in hunting which constituted the major means of food gathering. They were virtually preordained for domestic chores and for sexual pleasure for men. Other tribes often tried to kidnap them so they were kept under strict control They had hardly any rights. Both in status and treatment, they were hardly better off than the cattle.

Religion is, the faithful believe, the expression of the will of God. From its very beginning, it sought to govern the conduct of its followers in every aspect. The surrender to the will of God embodied in religion was by and large self-imposed. But its widespread acceptance must have at least been facilitated by the fact that it provided answers, satisfactory as they then seemed, to the various problems and questions that clamoured for convincing solutions.

Islam, according to the Holy Quran and the Prophet, is an eternal religion. But historically speaking, its world-wide acceptance during and after the time of the Prophet must have been for no different reasons. The societies as they existed in the then known world seemed as if they were awaiting the advent of Islam.

---

* Mr. Muzammil is an Advocate in Delhi High Court.

Presently, we are concerned with the impact of Islam on the status of women in those societies, especially in Arabia. How were the women faring there ?

Before and After the Coming of Islam

Arabia was at the periphery of the then known world which had been the cradle of some ancient and truly remarkable civilisations. But they had not been able to penetrate the vast Arabian desert which was inhabited by nomadic tribes. Even though the cities of Mecca and Medina flourished, the bulk of the Arabs roamed about in the desert. Inter-tribal rivalries often exploded in bloody wars. There was no education, at any rate not among the women. It was known as the period of *jehalat*, wildness, stark ignorance, Theirs were in every material respect pre-historic societies.

The pre-Prophet Arabian women had no rights. They were the absolute property of their fathers, their husbands and their sons, depending upon who happened to be at the head of the family at any given time. They could be married at will, most often against their will. They had no say or choice in the matter. They could inherit no property; they could only subsist as pleasure-giving, breeding machines.

The institution of marriage was, of course, not unknown but it did not confer on them any rights. The bride-money, *mehr*, was paid to their fathers or brothers. After their marriage, they could be sent to other men whom their husbands considered to be nobility, so that the husbands could boast of the nobility of their offspring. Before marriage, they could be made to invite young men, not more than ten in number, to have sexual relations with them till they conceived. When a child was conceived they could name any of those young men as the father of the child. They could be forced into prostition with select persons and when a child was born, the man who resembled it was declared the father. A man was free to have any number of wives, concubines and slave-women.

Culture presupposes a measure of economic independence and leisure. The pre-Islamic women of Arabia had neither. Tied down to the day-long domestic chores and prodigious child bearing, uneducated and effectively segregated from the socio-cultural mainstream, steeped in poverty, the women's plight was hardly better than that of their sisters of pre-historic Arabia. Time had stood still, as it were, for countless centuries.

The Holy Quran brought about a fundamental change in the women's status. Recognising and sympathising with their sad plight, it conferred on them a status far different from, and superior to, what they had, or for that matter, what their sisters in other civilisations were accustomed to. Though still deemed not equal to the men folk, they were nevertheless recognised as human beings and granted a good measure of rights, the foremost being that their infanticide was totally prohibited.

Rights in Marriage and Divorce

The Holy Quran declared that women could not be married against their will, their own free consent expressed in the open alone could bind them in matrimony; the *mehr* was to be paid to them and was their property. It enjoined on their menfolk to be fair, considerate and humane towards women. Their menfolk were allowed to have four wives at a time, to be equally well treated and maintained, the choice to marry or not to marry a man already possessed of wife was nevertheless the prospective bride's. If she chose to marry him, it was her own free choice, not a compulsion of law. But the consent of the existing wife or wives to the new marriage was not necessary; they had no say in the matter.

Once married, Muslim women's rights stand curtailed in certain matters. She can refuse consummation unless the *mehr* is paid promptly to her, but she cannot prevent her husband from contracting another marriage. The husband can divorce her for good reasons but since he is not required to establish those reasons before any earthly authority, the divorce can be at his will, even whim. The Holy Quran lays down that a divorce, to become effective and final, has to be proclaimed by the husband in three different gatherings in three consecutive months, but at the moment the declaration of divorce even only once, when communicated to the wife is accepted as final and effective.

Muslim wives have no corresponding rights of divorce. However, they can persuade their husbands to agree to a divorce on surrendering part of their *mehr*. They can obtain divorce through the intervention of the courts in the case of real hardship, like absence of the husband for four years when his whereabouts are not known, imprisonment of the husband for seven years and above, failure of the husband to perform his marital obligations for three years or to provide maintenance for three years and cruelty which includes the disposal of the wife's property against her will.

There is, however, one limited field where the wives have equal rights with the husbands to bring about the end of the marriage. The Muslim law of marriage, like all such laws, is hedged with certain restrictions and prohibitions like not having more than four wives at a time or marrying the sister of a wife. The breach of these restrictions renders the marriage irregular. However, the husband can validate these marriages by divorcing one of the earlier wives or the sister of his new wife. But before the husband validates the irregular marriage, the new wife is free to repudiate the marriage

Apart from conferring upon women certain concrete rights in the domain of marriage and divorce, Islam conferred on them the right to inherit and own property. *Mehr* no longer belonged to their father or guardian. A women had the right to inherit the property of her deceased father, husband and son. She had the right to payment of her unpaid *mehr* at the dissolution of her marriage at the death of her husband or by divorce. She had, however, only one disadvantage. Her share was half of what her male counterpart would get.

Progressive in the Past, Later Static

Women all the world over enjoy primacy in the upbringing of children. The mother's love and affection for the children is equal, if not greater than that of the father's. It is the mother who moulds the minds of children. However in Muslim law, on the dissolution of marriage by divorce or death of her husband, her right to the custody of the children except a male child not yet seven years old and a female child yet to attain puberty, is gone. She is not the guardian of her children; it is their father alone, if alive, who is guardian and thereafter his father and other male agnates, unless he appoints some other male person as such in his will. The deprivation is heart-rending.

The legal rights, despite the limitations, conferred on Muslim women more than fourteen centuries ago, were far ahead of what women in other societies and religions were entitled to until modern times when secular legislation enlarged their rights to almost equal those of men. The Holy Quran does not confer the status of equality on women; theirs is essentially a subordinate status.The evidence of two women witnesses is equal in weight to the evidence of a single man.

The Muslim societies have over the centuries remained by and large static. It is only recently that modern education and technology have started influencing them. The pace of change among the Indian Muslims has been even slower. Their being a minority has made them even more touchy and opposed to the winds of change. An ever increasing number of educated and working women is ultimately bound to create a wider and deeper awakening to their rights. It would, however, be counterproductive to speed up the pace of change or to look too far into the future. The impact of time will be far more potent.

CHAPTER V

Impact of Islamic Scriptures on the Status of Women

DR. MUMTAZ ALI KHAN*

The Theme

The socio-legal status of Muslim women in contemporary Indian Society is so degraded that one wonders whether this is what the Islamic scriptures have contributed to Muslim women's stability, progress and prosperity. To the non-Muslims who often show more concern for Muslim women's pitiable status, Islam looks male-dominated, discriminating against women in more than one way. In other words, the present Muslim society is equated with the Islamic society. But this is not the correct approach. Islam has provided a definite place, with assured better status to women and if there is any contradiction observed today, it is because of deviations from the Holy Scriptures, meaning thereby that there is hardly any impact of Islamic scriptures on the status of women today. This therefore demands an objective scrutiny of the social situation and the true spirit of Islam and remedial measures to protect women against the unscrupulous men. This is the essence of the theme of this chapter.

Women's Status in Early Islam:

To understand the present status of Muslim women, we have to trace the status of women in Arabia and the surrounding countries fourteen centuries ago, before Islam was born.A woman in those days had absolutely no independent existence. She was just a chattel, a slave. She had not only no equality in any sense of the term, but also no right to property, freedom of expression, dignity, etc. Her condition as reflected through the social order and social system was extremely pathetic and no one had ever thought of improving this situation. It is at this stage that the Holy Prophet made a very sincere and serious attempt to provide stability, safety and safe guards to women. He

---

* The author of this paper is the Director of Centre for Research and Development of Dalits, Bangalore.

emancipated her from several social and cultural bondages. He gave her a definite status in the society as a wife, as a mother, as a daughter and as a sister. He put a ceiling on the number of wives of man could have and specific conditions were laid down for contracting plural marriages. A married woman was assured of her rights to maintenance, divorce, re-marriage. Women were given the right to property. They were treated with kindness, sympathy and respect. They were encouraged to seek education and participate in several areas of activities considered to be essential for their development. Thus the Holy Prophet effected a radical social transformation, introduced a new social order and a new society where man and woman were more or less equal partners in life.

The Changing Scene

Marriage System

The latter part of the twentieth Century is witnessing devastating social changes affecting the status of women in general and Muslim women in particular. The three major social institutions, namely marriage, divorce and maintenance are posing serious challenges, crippling the backbone of women who are today in distress.

Polygamy is permitted in Islam. To some this has become a privilege and an unquestionable right. Though available research studies indicate that monogamy is still the rule and polygamy is an exception, it cannot be denied that even this limited prevalence has caused stress and strain in Muslim society. Contradictory to expectation, plural marriages prevail among the Muslims of the lower strata. The first wife is often unaware of the efforts of the husband to contract a second marriage. Even the second wife is not aware of the first marriage of her husband. Second marriage generally means negligence and desertion of the first wife and children from her. The husband is not in a position to treat the two wives with perfect equality. Instead of equality, the husband showers cruelty on one of the two.

It is true that marriage in Islam is a civil contract. But to say that it is not sufficiently solemn or sacred is a fallacy. The conditions laid down in Islam for plural marriages are so difficult to comply with that they amount to a virtual prohibition of polygamy. In fact, monogamy follows from a strict construction of the Prophet's own directive. Total prohibition of a second marriage is also not in tune with social realities and needs. Some circumstances do warrant polygamy. But strict compliance with the Islamic injunctions which attempt to exercise social control over men is to be enforced.

Desertion and ill-treatment of a wife even without contracting the second marriage are also on the increase in the lower sections of Muslim society. For months and sometimes for years the husbands keep away from their wives, causing social, economic and psychological stresses and strains. The Muslim society hardly exercises any pressure over such husbands.

The 'dowry' system has crept into Muslim society. Marriages have become expensive. Many customs ruin the marriage parties. All those have violated the great guidelines that the Holy Koran has held out to mankind to save women from decay and destruction. Islam provides for the simplest marriage. The poorest of the poor should have no problem in getting married. But the present day social order prevents this. Girls are either forced to remain unmarried or marry boys of other religions. Muslim society does not tolerate a Muslim girl marrying a non-Muslim: but it hardly exercises any pressure over the deviants. Dowry deaths are not ruled out today among Muslims.

The Divorce System

The second major problem relates to 'divorce'. Marriage is regarded as a civil contract and as such can be dissolved. The Islamic law naturally recognizes this right to dissolve the contract under certain given circumstances. Divorce is definitely a natural corollary to the concept of marriage. When the parties to the marriage find it impossible to lead a happy life, they should be allowed to break the tie.

But what we notice today is that divorce has become much easier to practise than plural marriage. Pronouncing *talaq* three times often consecutively, stamps the fate of the wife. Reasons need not be assigned. It is the pleasure and privilege of the husband. But the wife is flatly denied her right to divorce the husband (*khula*) until he gives his consent. Thus the suffering wife is put to greater hardship when the husband can take a second wife, ill-treat the first wife, all in gross violation of Islamic injunctions. There are instances where husbands demand thousands of rupees and exemption from payment of *mehar* (dower) from the wives in consideration of giving consent to *khula*. Islam provides for divorce as a right to both the parties, but to be exerted sparingly, as a last resort.

Maintenance

Maintenance of the divorced wife for ever or until her re-marriage is prescribed in the Islamic scriptures. The quantum of maintenance amount (alimony) depends upon the status of the husband, but quite often either the alimony is not paid at all or a negligible amount is paid. Even for this, the wife has to move the court. The husband exercises his right to appeal to the highest court of the land. He tries to take shelter under the Muslim Personal Law, attacking the Code of Criminal Procedure as un-Islamic.

Property Right

Islamic laws allow a definite share to the woman as a wife, a daughter, a sister and so on. There is no doubt that perfect equality between men and women does not prevail. But even the limited share is a great boon. However, in actual practice, attempts are often made to deny the sisters of their legitimate share under one pretext or the other. Poor girls become helpless either because they are reluctant to cause family quarrels or because of the difficulty of fighting the issue in the courts.

Other Handicaps

Besides these problems affecting the status of women, there are also other handicaps curtailing individual freedom and equality of opportunities. Women of the lower strata are often made to confine themselves to the four walls of the house, a stinking kitchen, a polluted environment, all leading to poor health. Pardah and Burkah are rigidly insisted upon without due care for alternatives essential for the fuller development of the human personality. The majority of women patients in hospitals are Muslims.

Family planning is discouraged on the ground that Islam does not permit it. While it is true that Islam does not permit killing a live child in the womb of the mother, there is no total blanket prohibition on contraception.

There is no positive evidence in Islamic Scriptures against the norm of a small family. But unfortunately some organisations give a different twist in the name of Islamic injunctions. Muslim women of the lower strata suffer today from bearing too many children — beyond their capacities.

A Caution!

The cheap jibe about freak *talaqs* and the helpless bonded status of Muslim women in wedlock are often attributed to discrimination enshrined in the Holy Koran. But this is solely due to ignorance of historical realities. We should have regard to the circumstances that prevailed during the pre-Islamic period in the Arabic world where sexual-promiscuity and social injustice played havoc. Unlimited wives, indiscriminate divorces at the men's pleasure and unquestionable and unbreakable chains for women formed the core of the then social order. It was at this stage that the Holy Prophet, the great messenger of God and revolutionary, attempted to plant certain restraints on the unlimited right of the male. He showered on women certain rights, though limited and cautious. He introduced an innovative rational and fair system. This attempt of the Holy Prophet was to modernize the social status of women.

Thus, the great damage done to the Muslim women's status today is not because of the conservative nature of Islamic injunctions, but because of the ignoring of them. The various un-Islamic customs and the Muslim Personal Law, the handiwork of the Anglo-Saxon jurists who misinterpreted Islamic injunctions while sitting in Downing Street in London, have brought misery to Muslim women.

The non-Muslims who raise the issue of the status of Muslim women often fail to recognise the values of Islamic injunctions which are relevant to modern times if properly understood and practised. There is no chauvinism or fundamentalism here. Muslims of today can come to terms with the contemporary world if they go straight back to the Koran and renew their faith and belief by seeking direct inspiration and guidance from it.

Remedies

All this calls for a serious dialogue among Muslim intellectuals and theologians. The present Muslim Personal Law should be declared out-dated and un-Islamic, and hence repealed. There is an imperative need to codify the law governing Muslim family affairs, and the Islamic injunctions without adulteration should be the basis. This would ensure the status of Muslim women in modern times. The much demanded, dreaded and rejected common civil code, whatever be the constitutional and secular forces behind it, is virtually unacçeptable to Muslims. Instead of wasting time over conflicts and prejudices it is desirable to start with codifications of Muslim laws based on the Koranic injunctions. All the misery noticed in the present Muslim women's status is mostly because of the lack of organised efforts to relate the Islamic injunctions to the needs of the modern society.

The Muslim organisations have done very little to launch a new social movement to restore the status of women and prevent them from falling further. Several lakhs of rupees are spent on innovations or construction of mosques. Several thousands of rupees are spent on lavish dinners and un-Islamic marriage customs. But very little is spent on education, health and other facilities to improve the status of women.

No one disputes the fact that three is an urgent need to improve the socio-legal status of Muslim women which is far below the standard prescribed in Islam. If women are given more than what is laid down in Islam, it will not constitute an un-Islamic act so long as the spirit is kept up. The wide gap between what Islamic scriptures stand for and what Muslim society is today needs to be bridged. This requires organised efforts to demand codification of the Muslim Personal Law by annulling the existing one so as to bring it into conformity with Islamic injunctions, keeping in mind the just and decent needs of the changing times.

CHAPTER VI

Muslim Women and Divorce

Dr. Ramala M Baxamusa*

Introduction

How progressive is the Islamic legal system as laid down originally in the Quran? This is a topic that is much in debate today; most arguments focus on the current practices which are retrogressive and thus it is commonly felt that Islamic law is in itself an obstacle to progress.

The aim of this paper is to show how the Quran looks at an important aspect of married life—divorce—and to show how progressive it really was in this respect before conflicting schools of thought reduced it to a male-oriented set of laws, proving a hurdle to women's progress.

Compared to all other traditional legal systems it was the only one which gave equal rights to both men and women— to dissolve their marriage when they found it was not possible to stay together after trying all means within their power to live together on equal terms. It insisted that marriage should be based on a relationship in which the man and the woman are on an equal footing. It stated in words that might sound surprisingly modern to our ears, that if there is disagreement, "the parties should either hold together on equitable terms or separate with kindness" (2.229 Holy Quran pg 90) This is the spirit that we are looking for today in our legal system.

The Quran believes in the principle that no human system of law can produce marital happiness but human laws may at least alleviate suffering. And when marital life is wrecked, the home utterly broken up by misunderstanding, jealously, cruelty, or infidelity, what greater boon can a wife have than the power to secure her liberty. The unfortunate position of the women of India is due to the fact that women, being illiterate, are ignorant of their rights, and men, being callous, choose to

* Research Unit on Women's Studies, S.N.D.T. University

let them remain ignorant. (A Fyzee No. 151936 P123 Journal)

Unfortunately the schools of Muslim law (Sunni and Shia) all over the world differ to a large extent in interpreting the Quranic principles. These interpretations regarding the procedures of different types of divorce have reduced the laws in favour of the stronger sex,— the male. They crept in within 150 years of the death of Mohammed, largely due to the interpretations made by the jurists as the Muslim empire expanded and social conditions changed favouring male dominance.

Various schools forwarded their own peculiar interpretations causing rigidification which still prevails. The results are a lot of complication and to a certain extent distortion of the Muslim law of divorce. The law today in India as well as in many non-Arab countries is quite complicated and partly distorted. Unfortunately laws are judicially recognized. This is creating havoc in the lives of many Muslim women and needs to be modified within the Shariat frame work.

Section I

Quran Divorce: Today in Indian society the divorcing of one's wife by using Islamic law has become an easy matter for the husband. However if one looks at what the Quran has to say one finds that divorce is strongly condemned by Islam. Prophet Mohammed strongly disapproved of it, declaring that it should not be resorted to unless it becomes impossible for the husband as well as the wife to live together under any circumstances. The popular pre-Islamic belief that the husband held absolute power to divorce and could do away with his wife at the slightest provocation, was repudiated by Islam. The same chauvinistic pre-Islamic beliefs are in practice today. Divorce has become easy and the man can free himself whenever he wants and without giving any reason. According to a precept of the Prophet, divorce was condemned as the most reprehensible of all things permitted. The Prophet is reported to have said that "of all the things in the world there is nothing more displeasing to God than divorce". (Malik Ram Baveja: *Women in Islam* pg 2)

However the Quran permitted divorce as a last resort after all means of reconciliation were exhausted as it wanted to avoid the great evil of marital discord, in which the very object of marriage becomes farcical, defeating its purpose by causing unnecessary strain not only on the couple but also on the off-spring.

Husband and wife are placed on an equal footing for divorce. Though the Quran permits divorce it insists that it should be used only as a last resort. A Quranic injunction reveals, "Retain thou in wedlock thy wife and fear God" (33:37 Holy Quran). It further explicitly indicates the duty of men towards their wives: "On the contrary, live with them on a footing of kindness and beauty. If ye take a dislike to them it may be that ye dislike a thing, and God brings about through it a great deal of good" (4.19 Holy Quran) The Quran also suggests the mechanics of reconciliation; it says, " If ye fear a breach between the twain, appoint two arbiters one from his family, and the other from hers; if they wish for peace, God will cause their reconciliation" (4:35 Holy Quran) Though the Quran refers to several causes which may propel a man or woman to divorce, it does not enumerate all the possibilities nor does it specifically limit them to particular cases. This is because the causes which generally lead to divorce are so varied that they would differ with each individual case. However the Quran does not permit any outsider to separate any couple who want to live with each other in spite of the fact that one of them has a certain defect; though this could be a legitimate cause for divorce in other cases.

Section II

Types of Divorce: There are different types of divorce and therefore different names for divorce. When the husband repudiates the wife and effects a separation it is called *talaq*. The divorce at the instance of the wife is called *khula*. Dissolution by mutual consent of both is known as *mubarat*. Marriage dissolved at the order of the court or *qasi* is known as *foskh*.

Let us look at the different procedures approved under the Islamic law for divorce. We will discuss only two of the procedures—*Talaq* and *Khula*, the underlying spirit of which can be utilized today in making the laws more progressive. The *talaq* which is pronounced by the man is of two types.

1) Talaq-i-Sunnah and 2) Talaq-i-Bidai.

1) Talaq-i-Sunnah:- The Talaq-i-Sunnah is the most approved form of divorce, where proceedings for divorce are started on a pronouncement by the man during the non-menstruation period of the wife. The husband pronounces divorce during three successive periods of purity. There is no sexual intercourse between them during the three month period. Also, if the wife is beyond the age of menstruation then divorce will be given at the end of three months.

It is the duty of the husband to maintain his wife during *Iddat* (the wife is supposed to wait for a three month period before she can have a relationship (i.e. marriage) with another man to be sure that she has not conceived.) She is supposed to live with the husband for this period, unless or until she has committed adultery when she is thrown out of the house. During this period if the woman wants to remain with him, she tries to win the man over and if at the end of this period no sexual relations between the couple have taken place the marriage is terminated.

If within the *Iddat* period conjugal relations have been resumed the pronouncement of *talaq* is nullified. If during this *Iddat* period the man or woman expires, the marriage remains undissolved and each member has the right to inherit according to the law.

If reconciliation between the husband and wife.takes place before the third pronouncement of *talaq* there is no marriage ceremony required. But after the third pronouncement if the couple decides to remarry then the wife has to marry another man, obtain divorce from him, and then remarry. This is *Halala*. (Zeenat Karim Ali, Ph.D thesis *Muslim Marriage and Divorce*).

This is done to prevent the husband from giving divorce too easily but the Quran has further indicated, "When ye divorce women and they fulfil the term of their *Iddat*, either take them back on equitable terms or set them free on equitable terms; do not take them back to injure them, or to take undue advantage: if anyone does that he wrongs his own soul.". (2, 231 Holy Quran)

This form of divorce gives ample time for the party to get reconciled and also provides a period for arbitration. "Appoint two arbiters one from his family and the other from hers; if they wish for peace, God will cause their reconciliation for God has full knowledge, and is acquainted with all things." The Quran further states, "But if they disagree (and must part), God will provide abundance for all from his all- reaching bounty for God careth for all and is wise". Thus this form of *Talaq-i-Sunnah* can rule out a hasty pronouncement in anger or divorce due to forces from outside as there is time for persons to reflect. Secondly during this period the *Mahar* can be arranged and there is time to take decisions regarding the custody of the children, their maintenance, etc. It gives time to the wife to plan and get her maintenance. If she is pregnant it is the duty of the husband not to divorce her till she delivers and to maintain her while she suckles the baby.

This *Talaq-i-Sunnah* is accepted by all the seven schools of Muslim law of the Shia and Sunni groups.

2)The Talaq-i-Bidai: or irregular form can be implemented by a triple or a single pronouncement clearly indicating finality.It is technically *bidai* (irrevocable). Once this pronouncement is made, even when the wife is menstruating, the divorce is final and the marriage is dissolved on the spot.The party is not able to remarry unless the wife marries another man and obtains a divorce.

This practice of unilateral divorce at one sitting without need of a witness has been rejected by Prophet Mohammed though it was permitted during the pre-Islamic period. He insisted on *Talaq-i-Sunnah.* The first Caliph, Abu-bakar, too supported *Talaq-i-Sunnah.* It was during the 2nd Caliphs period, (*umar*) that the practice of divorce became easy. Wanting to put restrictions on the misuse of divorce he permitted this unilateral divorce which was irrevocable, thus punishing the man and not permitting him to remarry his previous wife unless she married another man, divorced him, and then married her first husband again. But this act instead of punishing men and reducing the practice of divorce became a more accepted practice and created more injustice for women. Among many of Sunni schools of law especially the Hanafi, the *talaq* pronounced by a husband as a result of fraud is effective. If it is pronounced during intoxication, by force, or during sickness it is also valid (Zeenat Karim Ali, Ph.D thesis)

This *talaq* does not provide the *Iddat* period for a woman to be reconciled to her husband. In most of the cases she is at a great disadvantage as no arbitration is possible. She is deprived of her *Mahar* or maintenance. Because she is thrown out of the house and, in many cases, the man has married another, she becomes helpless. The children suffer the most as often they are thrown out with the mother. This right to unilateral divorce though highly debated by jurists was permitted. In many cases it does not insist on the presence of a witness or even the wife when it is pronounced. This is not in keeping with the spirit of the Holy Quran.

Now-a-days many of the Islamic countries have adopted legislative measures to deal with the problem through enactment in their constitutions but still many non-Islamic countries such as India permit it to exist. The Hanafis, Malikis, Shafais, the Hambeli and the Shiahs hold unilateral divorce as a permissible act, though they regard the exercise of such power without a cause to be morally or religiously abominable. (*Mohammaden Law* p.433)

The Khula::*Khula* is the right of the woman to dissolve her marriage. *Khula* means putting off or taking off a thing. That means a woman does not want to continue to live with her husband, and desires to be separated from him. There are a number of Quranic incidents (stories) one can trace to indicate that *khula* was permitted during the period of Mohammed and even during *umar*.

It does indicate that it is not a very admirable practice and the moral warning was that if a woman asked for a divorce from her husband without any cause, "the odour of paradise shall be forbidden to her" (5:277 Holy Quran). Her right to separate, however, was not curtailed. It was not claimed as hateful in the sight of Allah as *talaq*. However the warning is only a moral one. Some schools make *khula* equitable to *talaq* but others make a distinct difference between the two, "*Talaq* is the right of the husband whereas *khula* is sought by the wife. That while the husband forfeits the *Mahar*, when he pronounces *talaq*.the wife has to pay compensation or the release of the marriage tie if she pronounces *khula*. Also *khula* is an irrevocable divorce unlike some *talaq*.

One feature of this type of divorce is that a woman is free to separate herself even though there is no ill-treatment on the part of the husband,.if she feels she is unable to continue to live with the man. She has to pay compensation to the man in order to free herself. There are incidents in which the Prophet is reported to have recommended to the wife to return to her husband if he wanted her but when a woman refused to return thus, showing the equality of the sexes, divorce was granted to her (Zeenat Karim Ali Ph.D Thesis).

Today *khula*, according to most of the Islamic schools, is possible without the permission of the husband, and there are many cases where the woman has to suffer whilst the man can remarry and carry on his life without setting the woman free. The compensation demanded by the husband is also at times ridiculously high, though the Quran indicated that a man should not demand much and should free her on request. The compensation required acted as a check against the misuse of power.*Khula* is also not permitted by Shai and Henafi law without the man's permission. The other schools are more relaxed in this respect and permit it on payment of a compensation through a Kari. On that basis in India, the Marriage Dissolution Act of 1939, gives women the right to separation under certain laid down clauses. The freedom existing in the Qruanic period is still denied to her. Even today there are many cases where *khula* is not permitted though the woman has approached the court.

Section III

Law in Practice in India

Today in India we see that *Talaq-i-Sunnah* has not been used much in practice and the least-approved form *Talaq-i-Bidai* is more in vogue. The greatest defect of the prevalent Islamic system is the absolute power given to the husband to divorce his wife without cause. Giving of the *Mahar* to women to some extent restricts the loose use of this power but there is no legal machinery to force a man to behave and act as the Quran has indicated.

The Quran insists that a righteous man has to fulfil the following duties when he gives *talaq*.

a) A man is supposed to give his *Mahar* at the time of the pronouncement of the divorce.

b) Whatever gifts he has given at the time of marriage to the wife (jewellery, etc) will not be taken back.

c) A man is not supposed to divorce a pregnant woman except after the delivery. If she nurses the baby, it is the man's duty to maintain her. These injunctions have been completely ignored today, due to lack of legal machinery to put them into action.

In the early days of Islam it was not so difficult for a woman to remarry but today in Indian society where a stigma is attached to the woman if she is given a *talaq*, there is a great necessity to put some restrictions on the man, otherwise it really makes life for the poor woman miserable. The woman is thrown out of the house without any alternative and she is at the mercy of her family members. These days many of her brothers have financial problems and hence find it difficult to maintain her and the children. Thus all are miserable. The woman has hardly any property to maintain herself and no legal procedure can help her restore her Quranic right. There is no arbitration machinery to come to her aid.

The most important and dynamic law offered to a Muslim woman by the Quran, *khula,* has been distorted. Experience shows that much suffering has been caused by the husband withholding the divorce. It is necessary that this law be restored as in any other legal system and that this be brought into existence in practice.

Section IV

Examples of a few Jamaat Efforts: Today the different sects of Islam existing in India moved by the miseries of women, have been trying to intervene and search for some means of social control over their number. But they are helpless against the existing practices acknowledged by the prevalent Shariat law and the lack of any legal machinery to enforce the spirit of Quranic law.

The following examples will show that what has been done to improve the divorce laws has also shown the limitations of the measures adopted.

The Ismaili-Shia school has been the foremost in bringing social pressure to bear on its Jamaat members because it has a strongly centralised system. The Aga-Khan sect of this school has a marriage council to look into divorce matters and it has laid down certain rules and regulations. It does permit *khula* to a wife after all efforts have been made for arbitration between the husband and wife. Even if the man disagrees, it gives power to the woman to divorce him. This use of arbitration has reduced the percentage of divorce. But it does not have the legal strength to force men to conform to its decisions. For example a man is not permitted, according to the Khoja Jamaat, to take a second wife without the permission of the first wife, but he can easily get the Nikha performed by a non-Khoja Kazi under existing Muslim law because they are indifferent to the Jamaat's demands. Jamaat can take no legal action against him.

The Dawoodi Bohra sect of the same Ismaili Shia but Fatimi school has machinery at the Jamaat level which performs and dissolves marriage. A man is not permitted to give *Talaq-i-Bidai* to his wife. He has to approach the Jamaat and do it after arbitration in front of a witness. The Jamaat does intervene but little effort is made to see that the man performs his duties laid down in the Quṛan, if he *talaq* his wife. A woman too can also approach the Jamaat if she wants *khula*. The

Jamaat intervenes and can pressurise a man socially if he refuses to give divorce, but it cannot exercise legal pressure. In this case when *khula* is given the Jamaat will always see to it that the man gets his compensation.

The sects of the Sunni school are not as centralised as those of the Shias, but among them one does come across some action that has been taken by their local Jamaats. The Konkoni sect of the Shafi school is quite progressive and in their villages they do not permit unilateral divorce. The village Jamaats try to bring social pressure to bear on the man to follow the Islamic obligation as laid down in the Quran. If a man is outside the village premises and if he does not acknowledge the Jamaat power, it is helpless.

Even the Hanafi schools, which accept unilateral divorce more widely in practice than the *Talaq-i-Sunnah*, try and encourage *Talaq-i-Sunnah*. The Kutchi memon Jamaat of Bombay tries to intervene and insists on *Talaq-i-Sunnah* from its members. Again, if its members choose to disobey it is helpless, legally. Today, many of the Halie memon Jamaats are insisting on the *Talaq-i-Sunnah* being followed.

Conclusion:The only solution to the above problem lies in a unanimous demand by members of all sects to have a uniform *Nikahanama* in a contract and the necessary rights put for women into the marriage contract which automatically becomes valid as law. In the *Nikahanama* it should be mentioned here that the man would be allowed only *Talak-i-Sunnah* and the woman be allowed *khula* as prescribed by the Quran. In both cases arbitration will be there so that both men and women are forced to fulfil their duties as laid down by the Quran, whilst giving *talaq* or *khula*.

This can be achieved only if both men and women join together and see to it that such a *Nikahanama* is formulated and put into action for all Muslims of India.

This cannot be left to the free will and consciences of individuals to follow, because in present Indian conditions Muslim women and their parents do not have the bargaining power to include what they want in the *Nikahanama*, as they are many times at the mercy of the bridegroom. The Muslim women are as oppressed as their sisters of other communities in India.and are weak about giving in to demands for dowry Unanimous action by us is very essential.

Working out the details of the *Nikahanama* can only be done by women and men from every sect getting together and seeing that the true Islamic spirit pervades their laws and the injunctions of the Holy Quran are carried out. Islamic law can thus be made truly progressive, safeguarding the rights of women.

CHAPTER VII

Status of Women in the Christian Scriptures

JOSEPH VELACHERRY*

This chapter attempts to discuss briefly the status of women in the Christian Scriptures. By the Christian Scriptures we mean the whole Bible, comprising the Old and New Testaments. For the Christians the theme of the Bible is the salvation history. Except for the first eleven chapters of the Book of Genesis, the Old Testament deals with the salvation history of God's action in the history of the Hebrew nation. The first eleven chapters, however, describe what we may call the pre-history of mankind, before the call of Abraham, as conceived by the collective memory of the Hebrew people and of all the nations in the Middle East but refined in the light of the understanding of the writer or writers of these episodes. In the words of Blekinsop, "Genesis 1-11 is a sketch of the universal history preparatory to salvation history. It is meant to show the kind of world from which Israel came and in which the saving intervention of God was interpreted. By implication it attempts to explain why salvation was (and is) necessary." (Blekinsop et al, 1971: Introduction p.6). The New Testament is the continuation of this salvation history enacted in the history of the Jewish people centred round the person of Jesus Christ. The New Testament books contain the content of the preachings of the Apostles after the death and resurrection of Christ, about Christ's life, his actions, his teachings, and the teachings of the disciples and the life and growth of the early Christian communities in the then known world.

For the Christians, therefore, the Bible is the revelation of God's actions in history, and hence it is the revealed book. Revelation means the unfolding of the mystery of God's love and concern for man and his call to man to share in his life and share it with others in a new relationship, as between Father and children and between brothers. Thus it is the slow unfolding of his action, and finally his full manifestation in Christ. It contains also the reactions of man in the history of a particular nation, namely the Hebrew people.

---

* Rearch Associate at the William Carey Study and Research Centre and Madhyam.

As the word of God, or the revealed book, the Bible is an inspired Book. This means that the Bible in its essential purpose and meaning as a salvation history and message as intended by the writer or writers, and expressed in human words, in literary forms differing in styles and ideas, contains no error, or is free from error. This is the view of the Bible among Christians, hence the Bible is called the Sacred Book, the Word of God, and the Holy Scriptures. The Bible is the revealed work of God, and is inspired. These facts give credence to Bible and its authority among the Christians.

At the same time it is a human book, written by human beings, of different ages, from different places, in different languages, idioms and styles, differing in literary types and intended for specific groups and purposes, taking into account the contemporary experiences of the community in which these experiences and perceptions solidified. Hence it is the word of man also. To understand fully the message and meaning of the Bible, we should understand the *Sitz im Leben*, as the German scholars put it, the concrete existential environment and the historical situations that confronted the people and the writer.This is the task of the Bible scholars.

But the Bible as history — not in our modern sense — is the social history of the Hebrew people, their social institutions, and social life over a few centuries. The New Testament also depicts certain institutions and norms set down by Christ and his disciples and the life of the early Christian communities. In these writings we find the norms and the social life of the Hebrews and the contemporary Jewish people of Christ's time. Our task is to understand these institutions and the role and status accorded to women.

Our approach is sociological as it examines the group-norms practised, or said to have existed, among the communities of the Hebrews and the Christians. We are not taking a theological point of view, though it cannot be avoided as the theme of the Bible is the theology of the word of God in relation to man. The method we follow is the content analysis of certain passages in the Bible, analysis of the roles and actions of women and also the interactions of Christ with women in the events narrated in the gospels. The roles given to women in the society and the status accorded to them by Christ in his interactions with women and even that of the first disciples, give us an idea of the status of women in the Christian scriptures.

We will clarify the concept of status and role which are the key concepts in our analysis. Status is a sociological concept. It is a concept applicable to groups, and consequently to individuals in the group. Woman, is a collective concept, comprising all women of all classes and nations. Status, literally means, standing or position, coming from the Latin verb, *stare* (to stand). Max Weber the German sociologist was the first to use this concept to define the stratification of groups in societies. According to Weber, "Status shall mean an effective claim to social esteem in terms of positive or negative privileges" (Weber 1978: 308). Status thus means a claim or right to social honour, that is respect, or honourable position in society, which is accorded to the individual and to the group on account of certain positive privileges or prerogatives, or qualities, or due to the absence of certain qualities (negative privileges). The best example for positively and negatively privileged status groups in our Indian society is the Brahmins at one extreme, and the dalits, or Scheduled Caste at the other. For the Brahmins are supposed to have been born from the head of the Brahma whereas the lower castes are from the feet. One deals with the Vedas, rituals and so on, the other with dirt, agricultural and other defiling work. This was the traditional concept in India. And Weber applying, his concept to Indian castes, says that castes are status groups.

Status can be ascribed or achieved. The status of the Brahmin and dalit is ascribed by tradition, but when a dalit by his effort achieves social, economic or political position or any other than the ascribed status, he attains an achieved status.

Role is the specific social position given to an individual in a social group with reciprocal duties and rights. For example, the presidentship of an organisation is a role, and the person who occupies that role is a role incumbent. Roles can be changed, as is clear. Role performance makes the individual responsible to his group and thereby he achieves status in his group. Another concept which goes with role, is role-set. It is a cluster of roles of one individual. For example, an individual can be a husband, a father, a doctor, member of a club and a member of a political party. These are different roles, but the same person performs these different roles, as husband to his wife, father to his children and so on. Often one individual will have several roles, and the fulfilment of these roles in the accepted way gives and increases his social status in his group and society. We will examine the ascribed and achieved status of women in the Bible and the roles and role-sets assigned to them to enhance their status.

Now we will take up the main discussion on the status of women as understood in the Bible. First we will take the Book of Genesis, the first book in the Bible, and the first few chapters, where the narratives of creation, the fall, and Eve's motherhood are discussed. The first text is from Genesis. God said, "Let us make man in our own image, in the likeness of ourselves, and let them be masters of the seas, the birds of heaven, the cattle, all the wild beasts, all the reptiles that crawl upon the earth."

God created man in the image of himself,
in the image of God he created him,
male and female he created them
God blessed them, saying to them, "Be fruitful, multiply, fill the earth and conquer it" (Genesis. 1:26-27)[1]

From this text it is clear that God made man as male and female. That is, the social being man is male and female, or man and woman. No differentiation in rights or status. Man is not one but two, male and female.

The second narrative of the creation of man and woman, in the Yahavistic tradition, which is a simpler and anthropomorphic description, shows that woman was fashioned from the rib of the first man, for he was alone and had no companion. "Yahweh or God said, "It is not good that man should be alone. I will make him a help mate". So the writer says that Yahweh sent sleep to Adam, took out one of his rib bones, and fashioned woman as his help mate. The description brings out one thing clearly: woman is the companion of man; she comes out of his side; and stands by his side always. The reaction of Adam after seeing this wonderful creature was amazement, ecstasy and joy. He says, "This at last is bone of my bone and flesh of my flesh. This is to be called woman, for this was taken from my flesh." The writer adds, "This is why a man leaves his father and mother and joins himself to his wife and they become one body". (Genesis: 2:18-25).

The remark of Adam means that the woman is just like himself—the same species, unlike all others God created. Also the comment of the sacred writer emphasises the role of woman, a wife, a companion to man, and their life is one of unity and togetherness.[2]

---

[1] All extracts from the Bible are taken from the Jerusalem version of the Bible.

[2] Hebrews did not distinguish body and soul, as the philosophers did later.. For them body was the concrete living man.

The simple meaning of this phrase, image and likeness, is that God created them as erect creatures, standing on their two legs, unlike all the other living things which were either crawling or walking on four legs. Standing is a prerogative. Yahweh is the one who stands high up. Man is asked to be master of all creation and conquer it. This role of man, of the male and female is unique, for other creatures are meant for them to use and to conquer.Thus the primitive conception of man and woman, is one of equal status, and rights. Both are in the image of God. Both are of the same species, and they are one. The specific role of woman in these texts is that she is a helper, companion.

The sexual functions of the two differ as do the physical, psychological and social functions. The woman is called Eve or Hawah after her giving birth to a child and she is the mother of all the living. This must be after the fall. Afterwards, in chapter four, the writer says that the man had intercourse with his wife and she conceived and gave birth to a son. The texts show that the important roles of woman are wife and mother. She is the mother of all the living. Life was the most valuable asset for the nomadic tribes. And woman brought forth children for man to continue his posterity. In a patriarchal kinship system a son was the greatest gift, and Eve gave birth to a son. So she increased her status by her specific role performance. Hence the man called her Eve, (Hawah) the mother of all living. It is a role of honour, respect and social esteem. For a barren woman was an object of ridicule and contempt. Sarah had no child and this pained her. Motherhood gave the woman great respect socially, especially if the child was a boy. Thus, the birth of Ishmael increased the status of Hagar, the slave woman, of Sarah, and she was afraid that the slave girl would despise the mistress, so she ill-treated her. Similarly Jacob's wives, Leah and Rachael, differed, for Leah had children and Rachael did not. Their jealousy increased fearing that one would be preferred. (Gn 29:31-35). The laws laid down by Moses condemned the faults of children committed against their mother, as well as against their father. Anyone who struck his father or mother must die. (Exodus 21:17.) The Decalogue said that for a long and happy life obedience and respect to one's parents was necessary ("Honour thy father and mother") (Ex.21:17, Leviticus, 20:9, Dt: 21:18-21:27:16)..

The Wisdom books command respect for one's mother. Proverbs have exhortations to children about their duty towards their mother.The last chapter of Proverbs is a eulogy of a good housewife and mother, beloved of her children, husband and neighbours. (Proverbs. 31: 10-31).

The concept of status accorded to woman was quite high in the primitive estimation of the writers. Her status and roles were conferred by Yahweh himself, to be companion and wife to man and mother of all the living. Her roles increased her status in society. Now we shall take some of the social institutions of the Hebrew people in which women played important roles.

Marriage: Marriage in its ideal was monogamous, for it was so expressed in the second chapter of Genesis. Monogamy was the rule in the line of Seth, Noah's son, (Gen 7.7) though it was not so in the line of Cain, for Lamech took two wives (Gn.4:19). The patriarchs were monogamous, but they had concubines, at least those given to them by their wives. Jacob practised bigamy. So we do not find strict monogamy, but only relative monogamy, that is, a man has his legal and wedded wife who has the full rights and honour due to her. But for reasons of barrenness he may take another wife, or have concubines. In the later centuries during the Judges and monarchy, polygamy was practised. Moreover, the powerful people, like the kings, were allowed a harem. Thus polygamy was a legal fact (Dt. 21:15-17). A man could have any number of wives and a harem. Later the Talmud fixed the number of four wives for an ordinary man and eighteen for a king. These were abuses which later were made legal, for it was not so at the beginning. However, the most common form of marriage was monogamy. The books of Samuel and Kings do not mention cases of bigamy, except for Samuel, whose first wife was barren.

Divorce: Divorce was another form of abuse found in Israel. It was allowed and common among the Hebrews in the later period. We do not find it among the patriarchs. Deuteronomy allowed divorce, for mere displeasure from the man's side. "But if she has not pleased him and he has found some impropriety of which to accuse her" he could give a writ of divorce and it was valid. (Dt. 24.1). The schools differed on the nature of impropriety. The Shammai school admitted only adultery as a reason for divorce, but the Hillel school allowed any impropriety for divorce, say, even bad cooking. The form of divorce was to give a bill or something in writing to this effect. However, the wife had no right of divorce. But in other countries, such as Mesopotamia, a wife could divorce a man, and if she was divorced she had to be given compensation. It seems that the Israelite man could not demand back the *Mehar* (bride-price he gave to the woman and her father when he married her). Perhaps she lived using this.

Marriage entailed the gift of *Mehar*, to the bride. Thus Abraham's servant gave ornaments and gifts to Rebecca when she was bethrothed, and also to her parents. (Gen. 24:52.54). Jacob worked for seven years for Leban his uncle, for Leah and another seven for Rachael. (Gn. 29:15.30). David gave *Mehar* to Mikal (I Samuel 18:25-27) and Othniel for Caleb's daughter (Jos. 15:16).The *Mehar* was the sum which the fiance gave to the father of the girl. The amount could vary, according to the means of the fiance. This was no price or purchase but consideration or a token of joy. There was no dowry among the Hebrews.

Sexual crimes like adultery were punishable by the death of both partners. Sometimes they were stoned to death but earlier the punishment had been burning to death (Gn. 38:25). A virgin who was deflowered had to be married by the same man and he had to give her the *Mehar*. But if the father of the girl refused the marriage, the man still had to pay the *Mehar*. (Exod. 22.25-17). The rape of Dinah the daughter of Jacob was punished with the torture and murder of the Shechemites, despite the fact that the man concerned was ready to marry her and his father had promised land to convince Jacob and his sons (Gn.34). This shows the norms prevalent against rape were strict.

Slavery was common among the Hebrews and a father could sell his daughter to another man either as a slave or a concubine.

Inheritance. A woman did not inherit her husband's property unless she had her own, nor daughters their father's property, unless there was no male heir.

Thus in the Hebrew and Jewish society of the Old Testament times, woman did not enjoy equal status rights with man. In a patriarchal society dominated by men, they did not accord equal status to women.

However, some women played national roles and achieved national status. Esther, by her beauty and political astuteness, saved her people from the Persian pogrom (Esther 9). The rich widow Judith, by her sheer courage killed Holoferness, the Assyrian General, and saved her nation from defeat and destruction (Judith)[3] and achieved great status in Israel.

---

[3] The book of Judith is not included in the Protestant canon of the Bible, but is given in the Catholic versions of the Bible.

When we come to the New Testament, the first woman we meet is Mary, the Mother of Jesus, a simple girl from an unknown village of Nazareth betrothed to a carpenter named Joseph. The Matthean and Lucan infancy narratives describe a virginal conception and birth of Jesus. There are Bible scholars who see the influence of *midrash*, a type of literature in the infancy narratives, and attribution of virginity to Mary. We need not enter into the controversy, but spiritual virginity of Mary, that is, her total dedication to God's action and to Christ is more important than a physical or biological fact. Christ is more important than a physical or biological fact. The fact that she is accorded the status of the mother of Christ is important. She was a companion and wife to Joseph and nurtured Christ and stood near his cross taking upon herself the ignominy and pain and accepting the rejection of Christ by the Jews. This fact gives her a prominent place in Christian theology, spirituality and piety. Mary is the second Eve, according to the Christian theology, and is the mother of all the living who believe in Jesus Christ.

The norms set down by Christ and his disciples for Christians in the institution of marriage and family are important for us. Christ has emphatically affirmed monogamy (Mt. 19: 3-6) (Luke. 16-18) and says that in the primitive community monogamy was the rule, and no one must separate them (man and wife) when God has united them. So marriage is a divine institution. Divorce is not permitted and he who divorces and marries another is guilty of adultery; also a man who marries a divorced woman commits adultery (Lk 16:18). St.Paul exhorts the Corinthians that each one should have his own wife and each woman her own husband (I Cor. 7:2) St.Paul goes further and elaborates the reasons for monogamy and faithfulness in marriage because of its relation to the mystery of Christ and the Church. (Eph, 5:21-33). So marriage is viewed in terms of a sacred institution, where monogamy is the pattern, no divorce is allowed and mutual faithfulness and love is the sign and continuity of Christ's love and union with the Church or the Christian community. So in the New Testament monogamy is reestablished, is the norm, and no reason is sufficient for a divorce, except adultery, Mt (19:3-6).We conclude therefore, that the New Testament confers a new and higher status on women.

We may take cases where Christ interacts with women in different situations and gives them definite roles, showing thereby the respect, the status and honour or the esteem he showed to women. It is in group action or social action groups that the roles of each is defined, and roles are related to status. Christ in his public ministry and throughout his public life employed the services of women as his helpers, and close associates.Together with his disciples women also followed him and ministered to him and the disciples, and they did so from their own resources,e.g., Mary of Magdala, Joanna, the wife of Herod's steward, Susanna, and several others (Lk, 8:1-3). These women followed him up to Calvary and after his burial made preparations for the anointing of his body in the tomb.

Besides being his co-workers and associates, he gave them very important roles as the first witnesses of the resurrection and the risen Christ, and they were given the task of announcing his resurrection to the disciples. It was Mary Magdalene who first saw the risen Christ and she was asked to announce his resurrection to the disciples. After Mary Magdalene, the other women who followed him from Galilee also saw the risen Christ before the Apostles saw him (John 20:11-18, Mt 28:9-10).

The Apostles acknowledged some women as their associates and benefactors. For, in his letters Paul mentions several women who have helped him and worked with him in his different missions and journeys. Thus Acquilla and Priscilla at Corinth (1 Cor 16 19).

Christ's interactions with various women were occasions of revealing the various important truths he came to teach. Some of these discourses and teachings are the central themes of Christianity and the basis of Christian living. We will take only a few.

It is St.John who brings out these occasions. St.John is a mystic and his long years of Christian experience made him realise the inner meaning of Christ's life and its relation to our life. So he uses several symbols in his gospel as signs of a higher life. Hence his gospel is also called the sacramental Gospel. The first instance is the changing of water into wine at Cana at a marriage feast. Christ performs the miracles at the request of his mother. St.John calls the event the first sign Jesus gave to his disciples. A sign is that which leads to something more real, and beyond, that is to the new life, and Mary is the intermediary in performing this sign. Thereby Mary achieves a new status in the work of Jesus. (John. 2:1-11).

The story of the Samaritan woman (John 4:5-42) is the occasion of clarifying the new concept of Christ as living water, which quenches the thirst for ever, for it becomes an ever-flowing spring within the believer. The context needs little elaboration to bring out our point. The

Samaritans in contemporary Palestine were considered Scheduled Caste by the Jews. There was no interdining, inter marriage and even passing though their country was discouraged, as a spatial distance was kept. The woman herself had had four husbands successively and was planning to change the last one for a new one. So she was, (in our parlance) a loose woman, if not to say a prostitute. But Christ deigns to speak to her and carry on a conversation, he takes water from her—all of this shocks the disciples. Christ treated that woman like a lady and makes her his messenger to announce to her villagers about the Messiah coming into the world. (John 4:5-42). Thus for Christ there is no caste, no moral qualms, no untouchability, but only the woman, who is created in the image of God.

The resurrection of Christ was foretold and signified in the raising of Lazarus to life from his tomb. Jesus was the friend of Mary, Martha and Lazarus. In his journeys to and from Jerusalem he used to rest at Bethany. His love and concern for that family and their love for Christ, culminated in the fact of Lazarus's new life.

> If anyone believes in me, even though he dies, he will live (John 11:26).

The central theme of Christian life is revealed here. It is at Lazar's tomb and as a reward to the faith of Martha and Mary that Christ raises Lazarus and it is the sign of Christ's own resurrection and of all those who believe in him. Again Christ gives an important role to his two friends, to two women (Jn. 11:1-44).

We will take few of the signs and wonders Christ performed for the afflicted women. Luke the Evangelist narrates so many cases of Christ's favours to women. May be as a doctor he is interested in these medical cases. Christ raises to life the son of the widow at Nain. The incident is replete with Christ's concern for a widow. Her only son dies, and the narrative says,"When the Lord saw her he felt sorry for her". Nobody requested Jesus to raise the son. He says, "Do not cry!". and he raised the boy to life. This concern of Jesus is for the mother, who is a widow. Beyond a miracle we have to see his respect for motherhood. (LK. 7: 11-17).

There are the cases of curse. The cure of the woman with haemorrhage (Luke 8: 40-48). The raising of Jairus' daughter (Lk. 849-56). and curing the crippled woman on the Sabbath (Lk. 13:10-17). Jesus breaks the Sabbath to heal the woman, and the controversy it raised shows his attitude to people and especially this poor crippled women. He asks whether an ass or a daughter of Abraham is greater. He upholds the dignity of a poor woman tortured for several years.

All these and other instances where Christ deals with women are replete with the expressions of his tenderness, love and concern. His pity evokes his power and cures them. The narratives must be read to capture the concern of Christ for the lot of women in his time and for that matter for all women.

Now for a few of the woman who were quite on the wrong path. There is the case of the woman who was a sinner and who washed his feet and anointed them at the Pharisees's house (Lk 7:36:50). Christ upholds her action and eulogises her and complains about the Pharisees' snobbishness and high-brow attitude to her love and affection. Christ does not hate the sinners but loves them. He does not flee away from them but associates with them and raises their status before others. This is an occasion of another important aspect of Christ's work, the forgiving of sins.

The other case is that of the adulterous woman whom the scribes and pharisees brought to Christ at the temple precinct in the early hours (John 8:3-11). Again Christ puts to shame and flight those who accused the woman and had taken stones to kill her. Finally only the woman and Christ are left alone, and he asks her, "Woman where are they: Has no one condemned you?" "No one Sir", she replied, "Neither do I condemn you" (John 8:10-11). In this passage also the attitude of Christ is clear, he upholds the dignity of the woman, her person and life. One should read the several narratives to gather. the richness of the passage, the human compassion, concern, and the indignation of Christ towards the scribes and pharisees who by their causistry and hypocrisy have made the law of God void, and become inhuman and trampled down the dignity of woman.

So in the New Testament, Christ through his teachings, his actions and social interaction with women, and the apostles in their preaching, and close association with women as their co-workers, have laid down the norms of marriage, family, divorce and other.institutions that form the fabric of social life. The New Testament has re-established the lost status of woman in her roles as companion, helpmate, wife, mother and associate in the work of Christ. Thereby he has accorded an equal status to women with men, and fought for her dignity and social position.

Conclusion

In the Bible the original status of woman was equal to that of man, and a sublime one. For, together man and woman had to bring up a family, share the burden and master the creation. But this ideal got corrupted and women were accorded a lower status, and in some cases she was degraded. Christ re-establishes the norms and sets new standards and reaffirms her position, both at the social and spiritual level. Revelation is a process and it still continues in the Church. Liberation of man is the goal of this revelation.The Holy Scriptures have given us the guidelines. It is not only enough that each one of us is a liberated person, but we have to work for this emancipation. For Paul says, "The creation itself groans, awaiting the liberation of the sons of God," for in man is this hope. To be involved in the process of liberation from all the forms of bondage is the duty of every Christian (Romans 8:118-25).

CHAPTER VIII

Impact of Christianity on the Status of Women from the Socio-Cultural Point of View

DORIS FRANKLIN*

When a woman caught committing adultery was brought to be stoned to death publicly, Christ intervened and told the the accusers and executioners (all men) that only he who was without sin could cast the first stone. It is written in the Bible that they all dropped their stones and left. The original Mosaic law as recorded in Leviticus 20: 10 was, "and the man that commiteth adultery with another man's wife, the adulterer and the adulteress shall surely be put to death". But, somewhere we see that the law was watered down to condemn only the woman.

The writers of the Holy Bible, the scholars and the theologians, until the early twentieth century, and the makers of canon laws were all men. The very language of the Bible, theology, laws of the church, hymns, order of worship and the *Book of Prayer* has so far been predominantly masculine. Even Christ, the Jew, conditioned by the mores and traditional language of his time, used the exclusive word man in place of the all-inclusive word 'persons' or 'people'. When He fasted for 40 days and was tempted by Satan to turn stones into bread He told Satan, " Man does not live by bread alone". When the Pharisees tried to corner him on the issue of breaking the Sabbath, He said, "Sabbath was made for man, and not man for Sabbath" Again, this could be the language of the writers and translators of the New Testament of the Bible, but the fact remains that the message of the gospels, the good news of freedom from sin and redemption, has been presented to the world in purely masculine language.

The Scriptures, the laws—be they religious or secular and state

---

* Ms. Franklin is Editor of the *Indian Witness*, fornightly paper of the Methodist Church in India.

laws, have all been handed down to us through the ages by men. Except for a few matriarchal societies, throughout history men have considered themselves as guardians of society, truth, law, justice and religious orders.

It all stems from the concept that man is made in the image of God, therefore he is physically, intellectually and morally superior to woman, whom God created as his helpmeet. Thus, the sexist bias or sexual racism has its roots in the very thing called religion, which is belief in a divine or superhuman power or powers and an expression of this belief in conduct and ritual often involving a code of ethics and philosophy. (*Webster's New World Dictionary*).

The Creation Story

The creation story, as handed down verbally to the generations of Israelites and finally recorded in the first book of the Bible, tells how in six days God created the world separating the land from the water and creating the firmament, the moon, the stars and the sun, the birds of the air and the fish of the sea, the beasts and the vegetation. When He beheld his own creation He was pleased and said that it was all 'good'. He blessed all the living things and creatures and told them to be fruitful and multiply.

Then on the sixth day God said, "Let us make *man* in *our* image, after *our* likeness, and let him have dominion over the fowls of the air and over the cattle, and over all the earth and over every creeping thing that creepeth upon the earth. So God created man in his own image, in the image of God created He him; male and female created He them". Genesis 26 & 27, (*KJV*).The pronoun *them* could mean that all the other living things he created male and female but to have dominion over them all God created man.

Then God rested on the seventh day and blessed it.

How did God create man? In Gen. 2:7-8 it is written, "And the Lord God formed man of the dust of the ground, and breathed into his nostrils the breath of life, and man became a living soul. And the Lord God planted a garden Eastward in Eden : and there He put the man whom he had formed."

In this garden of Eden God created the tree of life in the midst of the garden and the tree of knowledge of good and evil. "And the Lord commanded the man saying, ' of every tree of the garden thou mayest eat freely. But of the tree of knowledge of good and evil thou shall not eat of it, for the the day that thou eatest thereof thou shalt surely die'." Gen. 2:16-17.

Though God liked his creation, including man, and called it all 'good' He felt that something was still lacking to call his creation complete. He named the man Adam. It is written in Gen. 2:18 "And the Lord God said, 'It is not good that the man should be alone: I will make him an helpmeet for him.' " The story goes on in Gen. 2:21 to 25 that "God caused a deep sleep to fall upon Adam... and he took one of his ribs and closed up the flesh instead thereof. And from the rib which the Lord God had taken from man, made He a woman and brought her to the man."

The creation story does not not end there. Adam called the woman Eve and they would have lived happily ever after in the beautiful garden of Eden, if Satan had not appeared to Eve and tempted her to eat the fruit of the tree of knowledge. Satan came in the form of a serpent and challenged the woman to defy God's order (why he did not go to man is not understood). "The serpent said to the woman, 'God doth know that in the day ye eat thereof, then your eyes shall be opened, and ye shall be as gods, knowing good and evil' (Gen. 3:5). When the woman saw that the tree of knowledge was good for food and pleasant to the eyes and to be desired to make one wise, she ate the fruit and gave it to her husband."

When God was angry with Adam for disobeying him, Adam made the excuse, "The woman whom thou gavest to be with me, she gave me of the tree and I did eat". God expelled both of them from the garden and told the woman, "I will greatly multiply thy sorrow and thy conception: in sorrow thou shalt bring forth children; and thy desire shall be to thy husband, and he shall rule over thee" (Gen. 3:16).

It is a Myth ?

The Bible commentaries tell us that some scholars call these original stories 'myths' but they are not myths like those found in classical literature—stories about the conduct and attitudes of the gods in their dealings with one another and sometimes with men. Also 'myth' suggests to the popular mind a story that is essentially fictious and untrue, whereas the origin stories in the Old Testament of the Holy Bible convey very profound and important religious truths. We may call them myths only if we are careful to define the term and make sure that it is not misleading.

"These origin stories are not historical in the ordinary sense. By their very nature they lie beyond the possibility of historical verification. Yet they are vehicles of great truth and should be read as such" (*The Interpreter's One Volume Commentary on the Bible*)p.1088

The Base of Concepts

Thus, we see, that the very concept of religious authority on the status of women is laid down in the creation story. It passes on from generation to generation and in the New Testament St. Paul, the greatest of the apostles of Christ, though accepting women as disciples, cannot refrain from placing them in the secondary role. In Ephesians 5:22-24 he admonishes the women, "Wives *submit* yourselves to your husbands, as unto the Lord. For the husband is *head of the wife*, even as Christ is the head of the church, and he is the saviour of the body. Therefore, as the Church is subject unto Christ, so let the wives be to their husbands in everything".

In his Epistle to Titus, Paul writes in Chap. 2:4-5, "that they may teach the young women to be sober, to love their husbands, to love their children. To be discreet, chaste, keepers at home, good, obedient to their husbands, that the word of God may not be blemished".

And St. Paul finally lays down the mandate for women to be in absolute subjection when in 1 Timothy 2:9-15 he dictates to women "to adorn themselves in modest apparel with shamefacedness and sobriety; not with broidered hair, or gold or pearls, or costly array, But (which becometh women possessing godliness) with good works. *Let the women learn in silence with all subjection.* But, I suffer not a woman to teach, nor to *usurp authority* over the man, but to *be in silence*. For Adam was *first formed*, then Eve. And Adam was *not deceived, but the woman being deceived was in the transgression*'."

Though Paul had seen the glory of Christ who, born of the Virgin Mary, had placed woman on a higher pedestal than the Jewish community, he could not break himself clear from the traditional beliefs and practices of his community.

Influence on the Church

Thus, the Church universal, with all its teaching, preaching and theologising about the ideals of justice, equality, freedom and grace, has been helplessly caught in a system and behavioural pattern which has emerged from and evolved around the age-old concept of woman being subordinate to man and man being superior, having been created in the image of God, the male.

The Church, from its very beginning has had difficulty in treating women as equals, and not as assistants and mere helpmeets and housekeepers. (Quotes from 'Good news and the Field to Proclaim it' by Zenaida P. Lumba, *Indian Witness*, Volume CXIV, April 1, 1984, Number 7).) Karl Barth, regarded as the most important theologian in Christendom next to Schleirmacher, in his discussion of the creation story in Genesis Chapter 2 said that the woman, " in her being and existence belongs to man; that she would not be a woman if she has even a single possibility apart from being man's helpmeet". This Karl Barth was the courageous defender of human rights during the Nazi oppression of the Jews, yet he could not break loose from the traditional concept of the roles of women and men. Aquinas went so far as to describe women as ' defective males.'

[1] 'Any woman who acts in such a way that she cannot give birth to as many children as she is capable of, makes herself guilty of that many murders...' *St. Augustine.*

'Are women human ?' (in the year 584, in Lyon, France, 43 Catholic bishops and 20 men representing other bishops, after a lengthy debate, took a vote. The results were 32 yes, 31 no. Women were declared human by one vote).—*Council of Macon, France.*

'Among the savage beasts, none is found so harmful as women.'

—*St. John Chrysostom*

'Women should remain at home, sit still, keep house, and bear and bring up children... If a woman grows weary and, at last, dies from childbearing, it matters not. Let her die from bearing— she is there to do it.' —*Martin Luther.*

'Women, in her greatest perfection, was made to serve and obey

1.All these quotes are from 'Should we be angry?' by Marie Assasd, *New World Outlook*, New York, January 1985.

man, not rule and command him.'—*John Knox.*

'The souls of women are so small that some believe they have none at all. '—*Samuel Butler*.

'It seems to me that nearly every woman I know wants a man who knows how to love with authority. Women are simple souls who like simple things, and one of the simplest, is one of the simplest to give... Our family airdale will come clear across the yard for one pat on the head. The average wife is like that. She will come across town, across the house, across the room, across to your point of view, and across almost anything to give you her love if you offer her yours with some honest approval.—*Episcopalian Bishop James Pike* (1968).

Christian Ritual and Laws

In the Christian marriage ritual the man is called the head of the physical body and the woman is asked to *obey* her husband. (It was reported that in her wedding ceremony, Princess Diana stayed silent over the word *obey* while taking her marriage vows with Prince Charles).

The Indian Divorce Act, based on the English Matrimonial Causes. Act of 1969, is applicable even today to Indian Christians. Adultery is regarded as the gravest infraction of marital vows and is, therefore, the commonest ground for divorce specified in all the personal laws in India. According to Section 10 of the Indian Divorce Act, a husband may seek divorce if his wife has since the solemnisation of the marriage been guilty of adultery. Whereas a Christian wife may pray to the court for divorce if her husband has committed incestuous adultery, which means with someone with whom he could not lawfully contract a marriage by reason of her being in the prohibited degree relation. If adultery is not incestuous, it should be coupled with other reasons such as bigamy, cruelty, desertion, etc. Adultery alone is not sufficient ground for a Christian woman for divorcing her husband, though for a husband, adultery is sufficient ground for divorcing his wife.

Among the existing matrimonial laws in India *i.e.* the Parsi Marriage and Divorce Act of 1936, the Dissolution of Muslim Marriage Act of 1939, the Special Marriage of 1954, the Hindu Marriage Act of 1955 (also applicable to Jains, Sikhs and Buddhists), the Christian Marriage Act of 1872 is the oldest.

The Church is just awakening from its deep slumber to the fact that for both divorce and marriage, it relies on the oldest Acts—Indian Divorce Act of 1869 and the Christian Marriage Act of 1872. This also goes to prove how heavily our Church in India has leaned on policies formulated by westerners for personal laws and church administration and church polity. In this respect Christians are truly backward.

Ordination of Women

Over the question of women's ordination, the Protestant Church in India has given its consent theoretically, but its leaves the women to seek their own fortune among the heavily male-dominated clergy. Women find that it is easier for them to learn theology than to do theology (be ordained and function as fulfledged pastors or presbyters) serving the pulpit and the congregation.

The Church in India, despite its seeming openness, has all its reservations to accept and honour women clergy (men clergy too are having their problems with the bosses). The few ordained women in the CSI, CNI and the Methodist Church in India can relate their own predicaments. When male priests and pastors are finding it a struggle for survival in the ecclesiastical hierarchy of the church, then what about those women who have picked up the courage to break traditional, cultural and religious shackles and entered the ordained ministry of the Church?

So far, I have in very lay language tried to state the authority of religion (Christian) on the status of women. But there are also those socio-cultural factors which influence and dominate the cross-currents in which an individual is placed.

Cultural Impact

The Christian community in India, by and large, is a product of conversions and mass conversions brought about by foreign missionaries. Hence, the Church in India is a conglomeration of both western and Indian influences. The early converts were mostly from Hindu, Muslim and Sikh communities. But it is stated that nearly 80 per cent of the converts were from Scheduled Tribes and Scheduled Castes. There are strong cultural impacts on the Indian Christian community or society which neither western theology nor imitation of western life style have been able to counteract.

Christians in India are basically Indian and their cultural behaviour, life-style, and mode of thinking differs from state to state and region to region, depending on the native language and customs. The Gujarati Christians differ from Bengali Christians and the Tamil Christians from the Maharashtrian Christians not only in their language, dress and food habits, but in their ways of worship and celebration of Christian rituals. But one common cultural image of a woman, which is neither Hindu nor Muslim, nor Christian, is that an Indian woman, though carrying the image of mother and goddess, should be in truth an embodiment of suffering, self-sacrifice and self-effacement. This is very obvious in Indian movies, literature and art. An Indian woman is overtly or covertly told that she is a true Indian woman (*bharatya nari*) only when she suffers in silence, toils and labours and serves herself last (husband first, children second). A very noble image, which many a woman has accepted as her sacred role and perhaps this is the secret behind many a saved marriage. But what has it done to women? They had so far ceased to think that they too had rights of their own and that if sacrifices are to be made they are to be shared by all members of the family. This has also led to male chauvinism and men expecting their wives to be co-bread earners but single bread-makers in the home.

Sociologists have defined culture as the sum total of the complex social heritage of a group which is created and transmitted from one generation to the other. As such culture includes non-material as well as material elements, its content ranging from the moral and religious values of a group to the physical objects a person uses to survive.

Every culture has its norms which involve moral and ethical values. Some of the cultural norms in India are respect for authority of age and position in religious or secular institutions, including the institutions of the family and the role of women in marriage, sex and religious rituals. Almost universal culture has destined women to two stipulated roles: procreation, motherhood. This has led to the following basic socio-cultural problems for women.

1. A young girl has to be married off. In the West, if a girl of 13 or 14 does not find 'dates' (boy friends who take her out) the parents of the girl start worrying about her and she is made to feel abnormal. To cut the story short, emotional break-down and rising lesbianism are the sad outcome of this socio-cultural norm.

In India, where dating is still rare, parents start worrying about the marriage of their daughters. The prevailing and existing dowry system among Syrian Christians of Kerala and the Christians of South India has many a sad story camouflaged by the glitter and gold of the dowry. Why is it that a large number of nuns are from the poor families of Kerala, West Bengal and Bihar ?

2. Status of a single woman: in simple words she is considered a freak. Accommodation is denied to single women. They are made objects of cheap jokes even in large gatherings and assemblies. Character asassination is their cross. In the West virginity is made a mockery of in commercials and soap operas. In India every single woman is looked upon with suspicion by men. Her very womanhood is under assault overtly or covertly.

3. Moral sanctions : women are expected to be morally upright both by society and the Church. When women are dismissed from service one of the strongest accusations is their 'scandalous character'. An unwed mother is put to all the torment and ridicule which a human being can face; but the question is hardly asked, "Who is the man?" It is often seen that the very man who makes a woman pregnant refuses to marry her. The prostitute is considered a scourge of society but hardly anyone bothers about the men who frequent the brothels. Society and religion both are guilty of branding women as the sinner (the Eve, the temptress, the Jezebel) and not as the ones who are sinned against.

4. Family upbringing: in an Indian family domestic chores are for the wife and the daughters. Men and boys are to be served. Thus Indian men have been traditionally brought up to think that domestic chores are unmanly and beneath their male dignity. This has given rise to grave tensions in families where both husband and wife work. The wife is more often than not pressed to hold two jobs—one professional and the other domestic. Men have been made to believe that they are the wage earners, but surveys show that the number of hours a woman puts in daily in cooking, washing, rearing of babies and looking after aged parents, if monetarily assessed,will be double the wages of the husband. Thus, the wife who is not employed is still a wage earner. Over the years her labour has

been considered her duty (*farz*) and not her contribution to the family. This has been the result of traditional upbringing.

Social Impact

Somehow the paradox of Indian womanhood is very striking. The educated woman in India gives the impression of a well-integrated and liberated individual. Women in India have been worshipped as goddesses and saints. They have managed the affairs of the State and institutions. Yet they cannot truly say that there were no social and cultural hurdles they had to cross. Also, they cannot put a veil on the sad and withered faces of their sisters, 70 per cent of whom live in abject poverty, slavery and, misery, facing desertion by their husbands. They have no recourse to law and justice. Their hearts and bodies burn while society twiddles its thumbs, not knowing what to do.

In the churches there is sexual segregation which makes women sit on one side of the aisle and men on the other. Though women are principals and managers of girls' institutions, their boards of governors and managing committees are nominated by men with bishops (all men) as chairmen. In conferences and committees men take the platform and women hesitate to speak—mostly due to inhibitions which culture and society have put deep into them.

The religious and socio-cultural mores and forces have played a demoralising and dehumanising role in the lives of Indian women. In general they have accepted that men are superior beings and in order to save the male ego and thus maintain harmony at home and in institutions they have to keep a low profile. This has led them to have a low esteem of themselves. While left to themselves they have handled their affairs well, but in a mixed group they prefer to take the backseats.

They do very well in their own women's organisations and groups, but in mixed conferences they hesitate to take the same lead. In the Church, women's leaderships is facing a serious crisis because educated women feel secure in the traditional educational and medical professions. They tend to give in to the power struggle by men, and lack the courage to fight against it.

Impact of Christianity

Though Christianity in India is dubbed as an "imported religion" despite its shortfalls, it has made a highly visible impact, especially on the socio-economic status of women. Though the Church, because of the theology and interpretation of the Scriptures has placed women as second class citizens, it has also never been able to quite justify the paradoxical image of woman as found in the Holy Bible. It is written that God created *man* in his own image, but the qualifying sentence is there — ' male and female created he them'. This means that woman too is created in the image of God.

God, in his holy plan for the salvation of humankind, chose Virgin Mary to fulfil his promise in sending the Messiah and the Saviour. He thus sanctified and exalted woman and redeemed her from the stigma of the creation story. In the creation story itself, it is the woman who dares God's orders. She and Adam did not die, instead their eyes were opened and they acquired knowledge of good and evil thus leading the world to exploration, adventure, inventions and innovations. Christ himself had said, " These things that I do, ye shall do also, and greater things than these shall ye be able to do". God himself released the human mind, soul and body to have dominion over the material and physical world He created.

At the time of the trial and crucifixion of Christ women were with him and they became the first bearers of the good news of his resurrection (the disciples, men, came afterwards).

In India the first woman's hospital and the first college for girls were started by two foreign missionaries—Dr. Clara Swain and Miss Isabella Thoburn. Both were single women. Five women in Boston, USA, picked up their support and they gave birth to the biggest ever women's movement, not only in Christendom but in the history of the world. This movement was called the Women's Foreign Missionary Society, of the Methodist Church. Through the efforts and generosity of this society, education and professional training of girls not only in India but in many other countries, gained momentum. In India hundreds and thousands of girls (and boys) from economically and socially depressed classes were given education, higher education and professional training. Teaching and nursing at first were taken up by Christian girls only, and they were socially looked down upon, especially nurses. But the Church opened doors for the non-Christian young women, and now they have taken up the challenges of these professions. Many Christian nurses have found lucrative employment abroad and have sent their earning back to their families in India, so much so, no one can say now that they were once hopelessly poor.

In America women are ordained as clergy and are given the pulpit. In 1980 Methodist women made history when the first woman bishop in Christendom, Dr. Mrs. Marjorie Mathews, a divorcee, was elected bishop. It was a tough fight, but she was elected on the 40th ballot. In the 1984 General Conference of the United Methodist Church two more women were elected bishops and one of them is black. The Women's Foreign Missionary Society is now called United Methodist Women with a membership of over two million and an involvement in ministry to women and children around the world, especially the Third World. They are putting up a strong fight against the arms race and nuclear armament. To us they appear to be very militant, injuring the balance in home and society, but they have ushered in changes and are ushering in changes, which after the growing pains are over, will give birth to a more wholistic home and society.

In India both in the Protestant and Catholic churches' women's groups, organisations and caucuses, are rousing their sisters from their deep slumber to awaken to the dawn of a new day God has given us. They are taking men along with them in their strides towards a more wholistic society of women and men.

A century ago our fore mothers stated,

> "So long as we assign to woman an inferior position in the scale of being, emphasise the fable of her creation as an afterthought, the guilty factor in the fall of man, cursed of God in her maternity, a harlot in the life of a Solomon or a Samson, unfit to stand in the Holy of Holies, in the cathedrals, to take a seat as delegate in a synod, to preach the gospel and administer the sacrament—the Church and the Bible make woman a football for all the odds and fears of the multitude.
>
> "The sentiments of men in high places are responsible for the outrages in the lower orders in the haunts of vice and on the highways, when in the marriage service woman must promise to obey, she is made the inferior and the subject of the man she marries, when the passages of scriptures are read from the pulpit they make woman a mere football of a man's lust... all our efforts to supress prostitution are hopeless until a woman is recognised in the canon law and all church disciplines as equal in goodness, grace and dignity with bishops, archbishops, yea, the Pope himself. We must have expurgated editions of canon and civil law, of Bible, catechisms, creeds, codes and constitutions and of Paul's toilet

directions as to covered heads, long hair, and sitting in silence and subjugation, hanging on man's lips for inspiration wisdom. The chaotic conditions of society can never become harmonious until the masculine and feminine elements are in perfect equilibrium." (Mrs. Elizabeth Mallet in *The Women's Question in the Light of the New Testament.*)

Strong words filled with emotion but not hollow words. They aroused the conscience of not only Christian women but women of other faiths. Almost a hundred years later women of the world again hit the headlines when they held their momentous assembly in Mexico City in 1975 ushering in the International Year of the Woman. Now the United Nations Decade for Women with its triple goals of Equality, Development and Peace, approaches its close. In July of 1985 thousands of women representing north and south, east and west, assembled in Nairobi, Kenya, to assess what had been achieved in redressing centuries of inequities and to plan future action.

When women constitute the majority in the congregations then why are they reduced to such a hopeless minority in the decision-making bodies of the church ? The Indian Christian woman, brought up under the prevailing religious, and socio-cultural patterns has lived in the false security of the male-dominated church and church-related institutions. She seems to have lacked the will to challenge the church and increase her participation in both the evangelistic and social ministry of the church. The UN Decade is over and yet the church women in India continue to passively accept their subordinate role. Most of them are not ready to go against traditional religious teachings. Therefore, relatively few women are searching for recognition and a new identity. But these few should not be disheartened. They need to take heart from their sisters in South Africa, Latin America, Korea, Philippines and Central America who have found a new confidence and are not only questioning the old religious and cultural patterns, but are bringing in a new order in church and society to build up a new community of women and men. The Church in India, awakening to new and relevant interpretations of its theology and mission, is open to discuss the issues women face, how they feel about their lives and what they decide to do. They have to plan their own course of action and action comes only from awareness—awareness of their status and being and awareness of the tragedy of sexism which has reduced a vast majority of women in this land to abject poverty and struggle for mere survival.

CHAPTER IX

Authority of Religion and the Status of Women in the Jain Religion

A. R. NAGARAJ AND CHANDRA KEERTHI,*

The Jain scriptures define religion as that which helps to attain spiritual upliftment, eternal peace and happiness during one's lifetime. *Satyam vada, dharm chara* means 'Speak the truth, practise dharma.' Religion protects and uplifts those who practise religion: *Dharmo rakshathi rakshitah.*

Jainism is a religion of non-violence, *Ahimsa Dharma,* which paves the way to universal happiness and peace. It is one of the oldest religions of India.

No other religion has given so much importance to human life as Jainism. According to the Jain religion even *Devathas* (semi-gods) have to be born as mortal beings to attain spiritual freedom. Thus Jainism believes that human birth is the first step towards achieving ultimate liberation (*Mukti*).

Jainism divides Jains into four classes: Rishi, Aryikas, Sravaka, Sravika, that is, the monk, nun, householder and housewife. Equal treatment is given to men and women in the sense that women need not necessarily be only housewives, but have the freedom to renounce the world to attain salvation, which some other religions do not allow.

Woman in particular has a unique position as Jana Matha, the woman who gave birth to the Thirthankara, a Jain deity. She has the highest position as the mother of nature, and as mother of Thirthankara. History is full of names of Jain women who have done a lot for society and their religion. They were great patrons of art, architecture, literature and social service.

* Mr. Nagara is the Chief Engineer Karnataka Elictricity Board and Mr.Keerthi is Deputy Director Town Planning, Banglore.

Noted for Scholarship and Saintliness

To show that Jainism gives woman a place of prominence and respect, here are a few examples :

Religious works of Jainism declare that whenever there are cases of fire, accidents, robbery or any such calamities, lives of women must be protected first.

Mothers of Jain priests (*Thirthankars*) are shown utmost reverence. The practice of worshipping the idols of such great mothers also exists.

The *Mahapurana* is the accepted sacred work of the Jains. It clearly says that woman has the same rights as man, to get educated, take up jobs and so on. Vrishabha Deva, the first Thirthankara, is said to have imparted knowledge of language and mathematics to his daughters first and only then to his sons. He taught the Jain alphabet to his daughter, Brahmi, thus the famous *Brahmilipi* is named after her. He taught mathematics to his other daughter, Sundari.

Jainism has given equal importance to men, women, monks and nuns. A contemporary of Mahaveer, Chandanabale, who was also his aunt, became his first disciple. She built an organisation of 36,000 Aryikas to help in propagating Jainism most effectively and succeeded.

Praises have been showered on Jain nuns like Kamalasree, Brahmilee, Gunamathi Sudarsana and others in the oldest Kannada literary work *Voddarathane* of the 10th century. These nuns were able to influence the social life of that period. Their characters were exemplary. Jain nuns in history have been known for their education, intellect, profundity and sacrificial qualities.

Among all the Jain nuns we have had, Yakini Mahattara was the greatest intellectual. A Brahmin Pandit named Haribhadra Suri challenged her to defeat him either in discourses or in theoretical arguments and if he lost he agreed to accept the victor as his guru. Yakini Mahattara accepted the challenge and she won. Haribhadra Suri became her disciple and later became a Jain.

Silappadikaram, a Tamil epic of the 2nd century, extolls the virtues of a chaste woman (*Pathivratha*). The story of Kannagi is of great value. This story praises the virtues of a Jain *Pathivratha*. Even now Tamil people worship her. She is known as Pathini Devi in Sri Lanka 3and is worshipped there too.

Political Leaders and Warriors

There have been many great Jain women who have excelled in the political field and also been brave warriors. Mrigavathi's bravery is notable. Pradyotha, king of Ujjain, declared war on Kausambi with the intention of taking Mrigavathi into his harem. During the war Shatanika, husband of Mrigavathi died naturally. It was then that she took charge of the situation. Mrigavathi, suppressing the pain of bereavement, spread the rumour that her husband was still alive and went ahead with preparations to defend her country. After forcing Pradyotha to retreat, she announced the news of her husband's death to the people. As Pradyotha's army was already tired out, they had to accept defeat. During the second onslaught from Pradyotha's army, Mrigavathi was able to build a fort around the capital and declared that if her son was made the king she would surrender to Pradyotha's demands. Pradyotha accepted this condition and Mrigavathi was taken to Pradyotha's palace. Instead of being part of his harem Mrigavathi succeeded in becoming a nun, with the consent of Pradyotha. King Pradyotha was greatly influenced by the teachings of Mahaveera and accepted Jainism as his religion. He then made women in his harem Jain nuns.

Kaladevi was the inspiration for the installation of the huge idol of Gomateswara. She was the mother of Chavundarya. Kaladevi's desire became a reality through the efforts of the great Chavundarya. Lord Gomateswara is hailed by one and all, from kings to saints, f.om litterateurs to common folk. Shravanabelagola, the place of universal brotherhood is where the giant Gomateswara stands.

Gerusoppe of South Kanara District was once a city buzzing with cultural and commercial activities. The coronation ceremony of Channabyradevi, sister-in-law of Krishna Devarasa, a king of Salvas, was a landmark in the history of the Nagares who ruled that area. The title Mahamandaleswa bestowed upon Channabyraden, the queen, was symbolic enough to signify how powerful she was. Edicts have praised the wars and struggles she waged during her reign. The kings of the Vijayanagar empire sought friendship and help from Queen Channabyradevi. There were many Jain temples in Gerusoppe and the *basadi* of Shantimatha Thirthankara was built during her reign. She ruled Tulunad for 45 years. She was a valiant warrior and died fighting.

Contribution to Art, Literature and Religion

Another great woman that Jains are proud of is Shantala Devi, who had the title of *Kalasaraswati*, and was the wife of King Vishnuvardhana. She had a special love for art. Edicts have hailed her excellence in dancing. She was a devotee of Jina and was well known for her tolerance of other religions. Vishnuvardhana built the temple of Chanakesava to mark the victory of one of the wars. At Belur, Queen Shantala built the *basadi* of Kappe Channigaraya beside the temple which is a rare event in history.

Christians have the Bible, Muslims have the Quran, and Hindus have the Bhagvadgita. Similarly the Jains have *Shat Khandagama*, Women played a major role in protecting and preserving this sacred book. The woman who copied the Jain scriptures in large numbers and distributed them was one Raviyakka. One edict, in the form of a poem praises Raviyakka's contribution to Jainism. She was a magnanimous personality who sacrificed her entire life in the service of her religion.

After the death of the great King Nagadeva in the 10th century, his wife Attimabbe performed penance for the rest of her life to save and propagate Jainism. Her sacrifices for the religion and her contribution to Kannada literature are of immense importance. The Jain religion rose to great heights during her time. She was known as *Dana Chintamani*, a title bestowed on her. She was already a widow when her sister committed sati. Attimabbe then took care of her sister's young children, who later turned out to be heroes. Jain temples of Lakkundi were built by Attimabbe. According to legend she is said to have performed many miracles. A few can be quoted here: She could put out any fire by sprinkling sandalwood water. She had stopped the floods in the Godavari by holding an idol of Jina. She made 1,000 copies of *Shantimatha Purana* on palm leaves and distributed them to propagate Jain culture on a big scale during that period. The great Ranna who authored the *Ajithanatha Purana* was her son.

The court of King Ballala of the Hoysala dynasty honoured the presence of the great poetess Kanthi. The literary duels of Kanthi and Nagachandra were very popular. People find them refreshing and lively even today. Kanthi was praised as *Abhinava Vagdevi*, by a poet named Bahubali of the 16th century.

One woman who chose to remain anonymous built five temples at

Mandharagini in Tumkur. She also built a huge tank next to the hillock, called the Mydala tank. This is not only for irrigation but also for water for Tumkur Town to this day.

Smt. Sonubaishah of Sholapur in Maharashtra started an ashram giving shelter to females of any age, right from a month old baby to an old lady. The women are educated in the formal sense of the word or given vocational training, according to their preference. The Government of India recognised the services of Smt. Sonubaishah and conferred on her the title ' Padma Shree'.

This list is not exhaustive. Each individual strove to further the cause of human service, to bring relief from pain, hunger, insecurity, poverty and illiteracy. The greatest virtue is the sense of sacrifice that is found in Jain women. They fast and lead simple lives. They were and still are responsible for the continuation of religious activities. Women have brought fame to their community. They have been wise guides to the men, preventing them from committing sins.

Jain women have shown greatness in almost all fields of social life and have brought glory to humanity. They inspired their men, and the old saying perhaps befits Jain women. "Behind every great man is a woman" .

CHAPTER X

Sikhism

P.S. LUTHRA

Sikhism is one of the most modern religions, not only in age but also in its outlook on life. It started towards the end of the fifteenth century, and its founder, Guru Nanak (1469-1539), was a contemporary of the Lodhi sultans (Bahlol 1480 - 88, Sikandar 1480 - 1517 and Ibrahim 1517-1526) and of the first two Mughal Emperors viz. Babur, Humayun (1525-32).

He had first hand knowledge of the religious and social life and political condition of the people of his day, and he compared these with the darkest night of falsehood, when real religion had disappeared and the moon of truth became invisible. To him there was neither Hindu nor Muslim, "*Na koi Hindu na koi Musalman*". Divisions and distinctions between human beings were all man-made. There was but one God and one religion. Bhai Gurdas (1551-1629) has in his first ballad thus described the condition of the followers of different religions in the days of Guru Nanak:

"There are four classes of Hindus and four sects of Muslims. In self-conceit, avarice and arrogance, they are wrangling meaninglessly. Ram and Rahim are the names of the same one God, but in ignorance, their followers, the Hindus and Muslims, have taken diverging paths, having forgotten the teachings of their Holy Books, the Vedas and Quran. They have been beguiled to the avaricious ways of the Satanic world. Truth has been left aside and the Brahamans and Maulanas are fighting among themselves."

Guru Nanak was born in 1469 A.D., and had an unusual childhood. Not being interested in his ancestral vocation, he tried several other professions, but nothing attracted him. He sought the company of Holy Men, and discussed with them his thoughts relating to God and Godly life.

To keep him tied down to the humdrum of worldly life, his parents had him married and two sons were born to him. In spite of this, he set out on long tours of search and study and visited the centres of various religions in India and abroad to see for himself the practical lives of their followers, in their homes and sanctuaries. He visited the Holy places of Hindus, Muslims and the Buddhists. He visited Kurukshetra, Hardwar, Benares and other places of Hindu pilgrimage in India, and went as far as Baghdad and Mecca in Arabia. He went to Tibet and China in the north and Sri Lanka in the south. We find it recorded in his biographies and also in his own words, preserved in Sikh Scripture, he felt unhappy to see how votaries of different persuasions had fallen from their religious duties and tried to show them the right path as he saw it.

The period of Guru Nanak's ministry was that of the enlightenment and education of the people. After him, the torch was taken up by his nine successors, Guru Angad to Guru Govind Singh, who completely identified themselves with the Master's teachings and carried out both in letter and spirit his mission of religious and social reform.They became one with him in spirit and so lost their identity into his, so as to become Nanak themselves and to write their compositions under his name and they were all thereafter known as Nanak II, Nanak III and so on respectively.

The institution of "Sangat" and "Pangat" — mixed congregations and inter-dining—started by Guru Nanak received full support and strength during the time of all succeeding Gurus.

Guru Nanak found to his dismay that woman who is an essential part of human society was considered inferior to man, and treated badly. He protested against this. He says in *Vara Assa*:

> From the woman is our birth and in
> the woman's womb we are shaped.
> To the woman we are engaged
> and to her we are wedded.
> The woman is our friend, and
> from woman is our family.
> If one woman dies, we seek another and
> through woman are the bonds of world.
> Why do you call her low?
> She gives birth to Kings and Prophets.

Guru Granth P.173

This Sikh doctrine brought revolutionary change in the status of women and they fully participated in "Sangat" and "Pangat" established by Guru Nanak.

Guru Amardas, Nanak III, strongly condemned the practice of "Sati", self immolation of the wife on the burning pyre of her dead husband and advocated "Widow Marriage".

> Sati is not one who burneth herself
> on the pyre of her dead husband
> Sati is she who dieth through shock of separation.
> Sati is she who bears the shock of separation with
> courage and lives contented,
> and embellishes herself with good conduct,
> and cherishes her Lord ever and calleth on him
> each morn.

Guru Amardas ordered that no woman devotee be allowed to visit him or enter Sangat and Pangat if she was veiled or observing Purdah. Thus Purdah, veiling of woman's face, was eradicated in Sikh followers.

Another hateful and heinous crime was practised by the upper class Hindus, it was "Female Infanticide". Some female children were killed at their birth. Guru Amardas, Nanak III, forbade this and issued an edict that his followers, i.e. Sikhs, would neither practise nor have anything to do with those who practise it.

With these injunctions and reforms, the women of that period felt much relieved and their status rose high and they started working with men shoulder to shoulder in the new society.

For preaching and organising his followers, Guru Amardas, the third master, opened 22 centres called "Manjis" and to manage them, he appointed 95 men and 52 women.

The fourth Guru, Guru Ramdas, gave the Sikhs a rallying centre by establishing the city of Amritsar and building a (Tank) Sarovar.The fifth Guru Arjan, the fifth Nanak, compiled the Sikh Scripture, the Guru Granth Sahib. He constructed the Golden Temple, the Harmindir, the foundation for which was laid by a Muslim Seer, Mian Mir. In 1604, he formally installed the Holy Guru Granth Sahib in the Sanctum Sanctorum of Harimandir. This Sikh Temple has four doors which symbolize that any man of any faith can enter this temple from any side.

This gave a definiteness and separate identity to the Sikhs. It then excited the religious jealousy and political opposition of the Hindus and Muslims. Guru Arjan was arrested and executed in 1606 under the orders of the Mughal Emperor Jehangir, as testified in the king's biography.

In 1606, Guru Hargobind succeeded as Sixth Guru. He wore two swords, one religious and the other temporal. He built the "Akal Takhat". From this time the Sikh Gurus became the target of royal wrath and the ninth Guru, Guru Tegh Bahadur, was executed at Delhi, for his missionary activities and association with Muslim Sufi Saints for whom the Emperor Aurangzeb harboured in his mind the deepest hatred.

Guru Gobind Singh, the tenth and the last Guru of the Sikhs, gave a militant touch. He insitituted the ceremony of baptism and created the order of Khalsa, which had to go through a relentness struggle for existence, out of which it emerged triumphant.

It will be of interest to note that when Guru Gobind Singh was preparing "Amrit" for baptising the "First Five Sikhs", the panj piyaras, his religious consort, Mata Sahib Kaur was present and she added sugar '*Patashas*' (Sugar Puffs) to the Amrit being prepared and remarked that these would impart sweetness and humility to Khalsa. This is a rare example in the history of world religions. Nowhere ever had a woman been allowed to contribute while establishing a religious order.

The successors of Guru Nanak, as mentioned above, accepted his teachings in full and made no change to them. They only lent additional support to them by way of explanation and amplification of his thought.

During his visit to 'Gorakhmata', now Nanakmata in Nainital dist., U.P., the ascestics Sidhas, followers of Gorakhnath, felt enamoured of his spiritual powers and invited him to the fold of Yogis and to adopt their garb. To him this was not the religious way of life and he told them about Yoga thus:

"Religion does not consist of a patched coat, a Yogi's staff or in ashes smeared on the body. Religion does not consist of wearing earrings or close cropping of the head or blowing horns. Religion does not consist of mere words. He who looks on all mankind as equal is religious. Religion does not consist of wandering to foreign lands or bathing at places of pilgrimage. Abide in God, be pure amid the impurities of the world; thus, you shall find the way of thy religion."

And at Mecca, the Guru told the Mullah Jiwan Sura how one could be a good and virtuous Muslim; He spoke thus:

"It is difficult to call oneself a Muslim unless he has the following virtues:

"Let him first scrape and polish his mind clean with the sweetness of faith (in God); and then faith in the leader of the faith; let him dispel the illusion of life and death. Let him submit to the will of God and with faith in the Eternal Creator, let him lose his ego and then be merciful to all creatures, then alone, sayeth Nanak, he can be called a Muslim."Let mercy be thy mosque, faith thy prayer mat and honest life thy Holy Book. Let humility be thy circumcision and cool headedness thy fasts, let good actions be thy holy places of pilgrimage, truth thy spiritual guide and kind actions thy sacred texts. Let His will be thy rosary, sayeth Nanak, then only He will preserve your honour as a Muslim."

It may be observed that Guru Nanak did not criticise any religion. He only criticised the ways of their followers who had strayed fom the paths of the religion they professed and did not follow the essential teachings.

As he himself came from Hindu stock, he knew about the Hindu society. He based his criticism primarily on their way of life, though occasionally he referred to others as well. He laid great stress on the practical side of life and attacked dogmatism and formalism and casteism. The conditions of the Chandals and Paras were the worst. They were not treated as human beings at all. A society which could tolerate such injustice, devoid of human dignity, was certainly not religious according to Guru Nanak.

The rulers proved no better. As Muslims they professed to believe in "Rab-ul-Almin", the God of the Universe, but in actual practice, the power hungry and self-centred Afghan rulers looked upon themselves as superior to their Hindu subjects and called them infidels.

The cause of all this, according to Guru Nanak, was the absence of the realisation of the unity of God in actual practice and in day-to-day life. The fatherhood of God was nothing but lip-belief with both Hindus and Muslims. Distinctions were made between man and man, between

Brahmin and Sudra, Momin and Kafir, and led to wrangles and strife. Unity of thought could come with practical belief in the oneness of God and real brotherhood of man could be created only through a congregation which recognised no caste or creed. This was the basis of the teachings of Guru Nanak and of the structure of Sikhism started by him and continued by his successors.

Concept of the Supreme Being

Belief in the existence of God is the fundamental basis of Sikhism. He who does not believe in His existence cannot be a Sikh. Guru Nanak has thus described God in the Main Theme, i.e., the Mul Mantra of the Sikh Scripture:

"There is but one God, who is all truth, the creator, without fear and enmity, immortal, unborn, self-existent. The True One was in the beginning, was in the primal age, and shall be in the future also.

He is neither installed, nor is he made by any one. The Pure One is self-existent."

Guru Nanak, it may be pointed out, lays great stress on 'His' unity and uniqueness. In his definition of God, he placed the numeral 1 (one) in the beginning of the first word of the Scripture. He further explains about God saying:

"There is but one Being — all pure, immortal, unborn, without any caste or entanglements, unfathomable and imperceptible to our senses, without any form or feature. Seeking persistently, I found Him pervading all the universe."

The God of Sikh conception is an existing reality and not an abstract idea existing nowhere but in our brains. "Our gross senses cannot perceive Him, our thoughts cannot fathom him, but our spirit can commune with Him."

"He is the cause of all causes. By his order all forms came into existence. By His order all living beings were created and by His order only do they attain to higher stages. All are subject to His will. The Supreme Lord who has created this visible play, sees perceives and understands everything and it is He who prevails in and out of the whole creation."

Incarnation Theory Rejected

God of Guru Nanak's conception was supreme, formless, unborn, and self-existent and beyond the intercession of any idols, priest or temple. All gods and goddesses of polytheistic conception are created by Him. The Guru, therefore, advises his followers to worship only Him the Creator. He said thus:

"By his order He created the ten incarnations, countless gods and innumerable demons. He created millions of incarnations of Vishnu. He created and destroyed millions of Shivas, and put millions of Brahmas on fashioning the world. My Lord is such a master. I cannot describe the extent of His virtues. "The Vedas do not know His greatness, Brahamas do not know His secrets, the Incarnations do not know His extent..., The Great Lord, the Parbrahama, is limitless."

Creation

Sikhism does not wrangle about the theories of creation. It is enough that we are here. The 'How' of it is not our concern. How He created the world and spread Himself is known to none. He Himself knows. Man is a part of His creation and is made in His own image. The Third Guru says:

"He Himself dwells in the body, but we cannot comprehend the Unknowable. The foolish and perverse do not know this and seek Him outside. O soul, thou art the image of the light. Recognise thy source; God is within thee."

Salvation

Sikhism does not hold out any alluring promises of eternal bliss or happiness on the mere adoption of certain rites or belief in any particular person or dogma but enjoins upon its followers to live a life of piety and virtue, not depending on charity, but as householders living upon the fruits of their honest labour. "They alone who eat the fruit of their honest labour and share it with others, recognise the right path."

A truthful and virtuous life of service alone leads to happiness and bliss. God can be served best in the service of humanity and humanity can be served by the cultivation of virtue and renunciation of evil. "The body is the palace and house of God and into it He puts His light. So nourish the body that you may serve the Lord."

"In the world we should live to serve; then do we find a seat in His court. Man's life is as his acts constrain him. What he soweth, so shall he reap. What he earns, so shall he eat. Truth is higher than everything except truthful living".

The Guru in Sikhism is the spiritual guide to lead the disciples along the path of God and Godliness. He is guide, a perfect man, who has realised God in his practical life. He, however, does not claim for himself any special position in relation to the Sikhs beyond that of a teacher. A Sikh will too also rise to the same spiritual heights as the Master, provided he faithfully follows the instructions in the conduct of his life and there is no difference between the two.

Guru Gobind Singh goes a step further. He says: "He alone is a Sikh who follows the discipline laid down. Then, he becomes my master and I, his disciple." Guru Nanak had, during his life-time, selected and appointed his successor and looked upon him as the future Guru of Sikhs including himself. When he selected his successor, he offered five Copper Coins and a coconut and bowed before him and declared him his successor, Guru Angad. The succeeding Guru, completely merged himself into the preceeding Nanak Guru and in turn became Nanak himself. This practice was followed by all the succeeding Gurus. The discipline of Sikhism, became the common heritage.

The followers of Guru Nanak and his successors were all known as Sikhs, including the Gurus themselves. The voluntary surrender of Guru Gobind Singh to his 'Panj Piyaras' to whom he administered 'Amrit' baptism, and requested them to administer him 'Amit' is in the history of religions. The strange phenomenon has been acclaimed by Bhai Gurdas II, a contemporary of the Guru, thus:

"Lo! There appeared an unfathomable man, wonderful, wonderful is Guru Gobind Singh—a venerable precepter as well as a humble disciple". Guru Gobind Singh forestalled his disciples from defying him by declaring in unmistakcable terms:-

"Those who call me God shall fall into the pit of hell. Consider me as a humble servant of His and have no doubt about it."

With the passing of the tenth Guru, Guru Gobind Singh, the office of the physical Guruship was abolished and the spiritual Guruship was vested in the "Word" (Shabad) of the Master embodied in the Holy Scripture, the Guru Granth Sahib. This gave permanence and continuity to the "word Guru" in Sikhism. Even when the Guru was alive, it was his "Word" in Sikhism that acted as the source of inspiration for the disciples, therefore, it is the "Word" (*Shabad*) that is Guru. "The Word is the Guru".

Every day Sikhs sing the following couplet at the end of their prayers. It is the Command of Guru Gobind Singh, to remind the congregation:-

"Command came from the timeless God and then was established the (Khalsa) Panth. All the Sikhs are ordained to recognize the Granth as the Guru. Those who wish to meet the Lord may seek Him therein".

To meet Him, who is unborn, self-existent, and formless, one has only to realise and feel that He is the creator of the universe and is present in nature through His laws that govern it. He must always be remembered everywhere at all times. This realization and remembrance of His omnipresence, called *Nam Simran*, in Sikh vocabulary keeps the faithful disciples always disciplined, alert and straight on the path. It fills a would be disciple with reverential wonder and inspires in him the divine awe that helps hold him back from drifting into evil ways. Constant remembrance of the Lord and of man's relationship with God and his duty to God keep a Sikh on the right path. "He whose heart is filled with the name realises the presence of the Master everywhere".

The Guru Granth, the Holy Scripture of Sikhs, it will be interesting to know, contains not only the compositions of the Sikh Gurus, but also a number of Hindu and Muslim Saints, whose teachings were in conformity with those of Sikhism. Guru Granth Sahib includes the compositions of five Muslim Holies: 1. Sheik Farid, 2. Bhikhan, 3. Balwad, 4. Sat and 5. Mardana and twenty two Hindus from all walks of life, without any distinction of caste, creed, high or low. The writers are 'Pipa' a raja, Sadhna a butcher from Sind, Ravidas a cobbler, Ramanand a Brahmin, Dhana a Jat, Namdev a calico printer, Sen a barber, the sagacious bards Kal, Gyand, Mathra, Harbans etc. from U.P., Kabir from Benares, Namdev from Pandharpur, Surdas from Bengal and Jaidev from South.

Unlike most holy books, Guru Granth contains no history of any period, race or country. There are no rituals prescribed in it. This fact alone makes it the unique Sacred book of all the universe.

Status of Woman:

The Sikh Movement had comprehensive, egalitarian objectives. Raising the status of women formed an essential part of its programme. The caste ideology had assigned to women, including those of upper class, a low social position. In some respects they were bracketed with Sudras. Guru Nanak declared: "Why call her low caste, from whom kings are born". Guru Amardas abolished the customs of Purdah, Sati and eradicated the custom of female infanticide. He appointed 52 women preachers to preach Sikhism.

The status of woman raised by the movement is reflected by the fact that they participated in the revolutionary struggle on equal terms with men. It was Mai Bhago who rallied the deserters from Anandpur and led them in the battle of Mukatsar.

Sada Kaur, wife of Gurbakhsh Singh ruled the areas which were under the Kanhiyya Misal. She led her armies in the battle and Maharajah Ranjit Singh owed his success in the initial struggle for supremacy against the rival Misals in no small measure to her political acumen and military help. Ranjit Singh married Sada Kaur's daughter.

Sikh scripture and traditions played an important role in uplifting woman's status. In the north, women lived as equals and subjugation of women after Sikhism began have been rare.

CHAPTER XI

Position of Women in Sikhism

Surinder Suri*

Sikhism originated in Punjab in the fifteenth century in the person of Guru Nanak. (1469 - 1539 AD). The emergence of Sikhism coincided with the upsurge of the Bhakti movement in different parts of India during a critical period of its history from the twelth to the fifteenth centuries. Although it is understood that the tradition of Bhakti relates to trends in Indian religious thought going back to the Vedic age and it is related to myths and legends of the prehistoric past, there were times, such as that of the middle ages in India, when the movement swept over different parts of the country. Of the original roots of the Bhakti movement, Dr. Sukumari Bhattacharji writes: "Bhakti (devotion), images, temples, personal attachment to one incarnate form or another, communal democracy (i.e. castelesness), ecstatic experience, music and the predominance of aesthetic ritual, dance—all these characterise the Vishnu-Krishna cult...Maya, the wife or feminine principle of Vishnu, took the place of Vedanta..." [1]

This is not to say that all the elements ascribed to Bhakti entered into Sikhism. But there is no doubt about an overwhelming similarity between the Bhakti movement and Sikhism, both in respect of the time of their emergence and their basic beliefs and commitments. The two historical movements are organically inter-linked. Moreover, the well-known Bhakti saints, such as Kabir and Namdeva, from distant parts of the country, are prominent in the Sikh scripture—*Guru Grantha Sahib*. Somewhat similar to the ethos developed by other off-shots of the Bhakti movement in different part of India—e.g. Sri Sankradeva's Neo-Vasishnavaism in Assam, or the Namdeva's movement in Maharashtra — in Sikhism too there is a blend of mysticism and pragmatism. The experience of identity with the ultimate or the divine, the ecstatic feeling of oneness with the highest reality serves mainly to wash away the prevailing rituals, customs, ceremonies, prejudices, etc. The human mind is cleared of the debris of the past ages and is able to look at the

---

* Surinder Suri is a social scientist who sometimes researches on behalf of CISRS.

1 Bhattacharya, Sukumaji, *The Indian Theology,* Calcutta 1978, p.313.

world around itself. Between the Vaishnavaite and the dialectically contrary Saivite tradtions, the distinction is made between Yajna, or sacrifice, and Puja, or ritual worship. However, in the Bhakti tradition Yajna is equated with self-effacement of the ego. The devotee becomes one with the divine or the ultimate, to be sure as an infinitesimal or at best a modest component of the ultimate. Another important point from the perspective of our particular theme is that the ecstatic experience is often identified with the male-female union. The disciple is like the female who unites with the ultimate or the divine. Needless to say that the ultimate or absolute or divine in Bhakti is not the monotheistic God, but it is formless, indefinable—at once nothing and yet everything. Hence it cannot be represented pictorially or materially, nor can it be idolised which would lead to its ritual worship. It can only be represented by a name, an abstract symbol but no concrete manifestation. Recitation of the name which is worship is really concentration on the nameless and the formless, although ritualisation in this sense has not been avoided in the course of time.

It is only fair to point out the ultimate is also sexless, certainly not differentiated into parts, without which sexuality is not possible. In this sense the question whether the ultimate divinity is seemingly male or female does not arise. There is no theological sanction in the Bhakti tradition for any particular form of man-woman relations or for any specific position for woman. As embodiment and articulation of the divine, in however limited a form, it is up to the individual to make a decision in this matter as in others. Whatever is realistic, rational and fair has divine sanction. So it becomes the responsibility of the enlightened individual — or the learner or disciple of the divine reality, the *Shishu* or *Sikh* to subject the prevailing customs, habits, traditions and rituals to critical appraisal and to sweep away whatever is unnecessary, unworthy of the devinely enlightened humans, or unfair and improper. Thus, the major thrust of Sikhism in its initial phase has been essentially the cleaining up of the accumulated traditions and rituals. Many of these concerned women and these are examined critically by the Sikh Gurus. A point worth making here is that there is no presumption about the status of women according to Sikhism, nor on any other secular issue; in fact only the pre-existing social presumptions are negated. From a theological perspective, the basic dictum, the starting point of the Sikh faith is the maxim that "There is no Hindu, there is no Muslim." In other words, all the pre-existing religious categories are rejected, as are the caste categories. There are no generalisations such as all men are created equal, or that men and women are equal, or unequal. In that sense Sikhism is not dogmatic, whether in the good sense of the term or in its derogatory sense. As a recent, unpublished study points out, "To affirm the dignity of the human being, male or female, brushing aside all the disabilities built up through the ages by creeds and social systems was at the centre of the teaching of Guru Nanak. In his teaching the mystic vision of the immanence of the creator is that all creation inevitably leads to the gospel of innate equality, felt spiritually... It would be unhistorical to look into such teaching for anything like the impulse towards the modern kind of democracy with all its implications. Sikh society, as a result of the emancipating teaching of Guru Nanak is in many respects the least tied down to tradition, and has been the earliest to shed the dead-wood of medievalism and primitivism that clings to an overwhelmingly large part of the Indian humanity...." In other words, the emergence of Sikhism was like a revolutionary explosion that delegitimised the pre-existing centres of authority; it then faced the task of creating a new social order. The two tasks are distinct but interlinked. So far as the status of women is concerned, it is determined in Sikhism, in Sikh tradition and in contemporary Sikh society by both these processes—the revolutionary as well as the reconstructive one. Determination of the status and position of women occupies an important place in the rituals and traditions of the pre-revolutionary orthodox Indian society. In sweeping these away, the status of woman is also redefined, or redetermined, even if in an indirect manner. Nor is it surprising that many of the rituals and traditions that were noticed and criticised by the Gurus, particularly by Guru Nanak, had to do with domestic taboos, practices and beliefs.

One of the taboos mentioned in the sacred book concerns the way in which a house is treated as polluted for a number of days, generally for forty days, after a child is born in it. Of course, the defilement is attributed primarily to the mother. On this custom Guru Nanak pronounced as follows:

> If it should be believed that birth renders a place impure,
> then it should be known that births take place everywhere
> and all the time.
> Cow-dung is treated as pure but breeds maggots;
> Every grain of foodstuff contains worms.
> Water is something alive for it imparts life to vegetation,
> When the kitchen is full of such births but is considered
> clean, how can we treat human birth as defiling.
> Saith Nanak, defilement is not washed away by rituals;
> Enlightenment of the soul alone purifies it. (*Asa di Vaar*).

That statement is important because women are often treated as the carriers of impurity; menstruation is generally treated in this manner. Although not necessarily motivated by the aim of raising the status of women in a direct way, the perspective has the same impact. As Guru Nanak added:

> Birth and death occur by divine decree; creatures
> enter life and leave it as God wills.
> Food with which God blesses man is pure.
> Saith Nanak: No impurity attaches to those enlightened
> by God's grace. (*Asa di Var*)

Women were considered impure when they gave birth to a child, but this natural or divine act could not be considered polluting. A generalisation is drawn that even the most saintly individuals are born of women and it could not be treated as an event bordering on sin:

> Man is born of woman, develops from the foetus in her womb:
> He marries a woman:
> Life's activities depend upon woman, who is
> man's true companion.
> If he looses a woman, he seeks another.
> He can be moral only if he is faithful to his wife.
> Such is the place of woman.
> The great ones of this earth are both of her;
> so how can we talk of her contemptously!
> Woman is born out of woman.
> None is born but of woman.
> God alone is eternal and hence unborn.
> Saith Nanak; that mouth alone is blessed which
> utters words of devotion to God;
> only their faces glow with bliss at the Divine Assembly.
> (*Asa di Var*)

Two points need to be mentioned in this connection. There is no attempt to evade the reality—birth is reality and each one is born of woman: even the highest and the noblest ones. To consider child-birth as polluting is to tarnish every woman or man, however saintly or exalted. Implicit in the perspective outlined in the above statements is that the status and position of a woman and our treatment of her cannot be separated from the status and position of man, however saintly or wicked. At a more metaphysical level it is argued that if birth can be treated as polluting and defiling, then everything, everywhere is impure, for something or other breeds everywhere all the time. In other words, human and social processess are interrelated with the natural ones, so that the hierarchy of different levels of nature and society is broken down. A similar set of values are preached for woman as for man:

Some women seek beauty and indulge in pleasures
Eat betel leaves, use the fragrance of flowers, and
chase pleasures of the flesh;
But these are like diseases of the spirit.
Pleasures soon produce suffering;
They alone find fulfillment who seek refuge in God.
O thou, my daughter princess!
Meditate on the True Name,
Make thy life fruitful;
Get rid of the lust for worldly pleasures;
Meditate on the Divine word.

(*Raag Basant*)

The noble and pious path is the same for man and woman though their tasks and roles are different. On the one hand, there is acceptance of life and the world of one's responsibilities and tasks according to one's capabilities; on the other, however, there is a balancing of the worldliness with the spiritually more important task of maintaining and strengthening one's relationship with the ultimate or divine reality. The worldly pleasures should not become overwhelming. Women should see to it that they do not become instruments of an unbalanced worldly way of life. Thus, Sita the ideal of womanhood in Indian society, is accepted as such in the Sikh scriptures: "the embodiment of all praiseworthy qualities and inexpressible spiritual beauty." (*Jap*). Women are asked to follow the path of devotion:

God asks the happily married wife,
how she and her husband have a joyful life;
(She said)
Through the decorative ornaments of mental
poise, contentment, sweet speech.

(*Adi Granth*, p.17)

A woman who is abandoned, what life does

she have?
She is miserable, wears soiled clothes
Her nights pass in agony.

(*Adi Granth*, p.72)

It is also pointed out that Guru Nanak, who wandered all over India and even outside, nevertheless led a happy domestic life. He is portrayed as very close to his mother, his sister and his wife. Renunciation is to him not the way to overcome desires. Renunciation of sex does not dim the passion:

By living away from human concourse, one sheds
not the slumber of ignorance,
nor does one outgrow temptation of lust for women.
Without absorption in God, mind does not find
rest nor is desire stilled;
Lord created for me seclusion in my own
hearth;
In following the eternal, amidst normal living,
is the true commerce with God.
Nanak, with sleep abridged and spare diet
can contemplate the Essence.

(*Siddha Goshti*)

There is emphasis upon self-restraint and continence, so that men should look at women, however attractive, as primarily either sisters, daughters or mothers (except the woman whom one marries, but she is also mother of one's children). This excludes a purely romantic or erotic society. Thus, the Sikh saint, Bhai Gurdas, in his *Vaar* emphasises:

He who forsakes father and mother, and yet listens to
religious scriptures, is ignorant of the core of
religion;
He, performing austere rituals, wanders in
wasteland;
God does not accept his prayers;
His ablutions at the sixty-eight sacred bathing
places do not win him release from the cycle of
birth and death;
His charities, as those of a misguided person, are not accepted;
His fasts and vigils are all delusion, annulling not
his karmic cycle;

He does not know the way of Guru or God.

In other words, the primary social reality is the family. If one runs away or escapes from this obligation, one commits the equivalent of the original sin. It follows that the place of woman—often treated as the core of familial or worldly relations—is central to Sikh piety. She should not be treated as an object of lust nor should one run away from her.

To argue that Sikhism stands for the equality of men and women would reduce the relationship between the sexes to that of an ideology in the Marxian sense. Such ideological equality merely covers up inequality. The true equality is to be oneself; however, one should not use the term equality for it. It is real freedom that is important, genuine self-realisation. Even though in the Sikh doctrine the relationship to the basic ultimate reality or divinity is central, it makes each person responsible for dealing effectively with the worldly reality. Woman therefore, is a colleague and comrade in the worldly as well as in the other-worldly endeavours.

Starting as a faith that had many similarities to the Bhakti-Vaishanavite tradition and movement of the middle ages, Sikhism underwent an evolution and transformation that affected the status of women. Perhaps the transformation of Sikhism, as it began with Guru Nanak can be illustrated by comparing it with the credo and life-commitment of the tenth Guru, Guru Gobind Singh, in whose actions and preaching the emphasis was increasingly upon Shiva the great rival as well as anti-thesis of Vishnu in the Hindu pantheon. Vishnu is contemplative, mystical. Shiva is an activist, indeed warlike. Vishnu has no enemies to speak of; Shiva is being attacked continuously and is fighting back. More important for our theme is the fact whereas Vishnu is only infrequently linked with a female deity, Shiva is inseparable from his feminine counterparts—Parvati, Kali, Durga. These feminine fellow-deities (with some of whom Shiva produced progeny) in fact represent cosmic energy, namely, Shakti. Tradition has it that in desperation after the slaughter of his four young sons and innumerable followers, Guru Govind Singh prayed to the goddess Durga for succour, and she gave him her arms. These arms symbolise the Khanda—a dagger, a scimitar, two swords—which have become the emblem of the militant Sikhs—the Khalsa. In the same direction, in order to draw upon the primeaval energy or Shakti, the Sikhs started to grow their hair and act as saint-soldiers: ascetics willing to sacrifice their all for the sake of their ideals. Sikhism moved not so much in terms of the scriptures, which remain primarily the work of Guru Nanak, but in practice towards some sort of ritualisation, as in the worship of the holy scriptures. The ideal of Durga—the warrior and invincible goddess—affected the postion of women in Sikh tradition. Woman became the co-fighter. The implicit image of woman in the early part of the Sikh tradition was that of mother, and the wives of the Gurus themselves were and are known as "Mata" or mother. After Guru Govind Singh's demise in 1708, for nearly fifty years his widow, Mata Sundari remained the spiritual and secular leader. Tradition has it that during this period of fierce persecution of Sikhs, thousands of women fought alongside the men. The tradition lingers. Similarly, it is believed that when Sikh warriors defeated their enemies, they never mistreated or molested women of their enemies. However, the nature of everyday reality shifted the image of woman from that of mother to companion in struggle. There are also legends of women heroes who led armed Sikhs into battle. The subordination of women to men symbolised in the self-immolation of a widow in the form of Sattee, is expressly forbidden in the Sikh religion. A women who thus burns herself, wrote the fifth Guru Arjun, " Shall not find union with her lord, but wander about in the cycle of birth and death." But a woman who is well-disciplined and obeys her beloved husband will not be subjected to ill-treatment even after her death. It is a said in the scriptures,

> The true Satees are not they who burn
> themselves on their husbands' funeral pyre.
> The real Sattees are not they who patiently
> bear the pains of separation from their beloved.
> The real Sattees are they who live the lives
> of sweet self-discipline,
> serve their lord and bear his memory
> in their hearts forever.

(*Adi Granth* p.787)

The ideal picture painted in Sikh scriptures, (even though there was a profound transformation of the faith between the first Guru and the tenth Guru,) had to adapt to the compulsions of society when Sikhism became a mass religion in the later part of the eighteenth and early part of the nineteenth century. Perhaps the major reason for the wider acceptance of the faith was that, with the decline of the Mugul empire, the effort to exterminate the Sikhs came to a halt and Sikh warriors were able to establish a number of principalities most of which were finally brought under the rule of Maharaja Ranjit Singh. There were other Sikh kingdoms, pre-eminently those of Patiala, Nabha, Faridkot. However, those who became Sikh were mainly members of the armed forces, recruited from the peasantry. Military officers and courtiers were granted estates. This process has been called "the feudalisation of Sikhism." When Punjab came under British rule in the mid-nineteenth century, Sikh armies were incorporated into the imperial military organisation. As a militant religious community, the Sikhs were favoured by the British and then religion was fostered under official patronage. In a way, therefore, the transformation of Sikhism that had commenced under the Gurus and was consummated by Guru Gobind Singh continued to spread afterwards, particularly under Maharaja Ranjit Singh and the British rule. The status of Sikh women became that of the soldier's wife. Some element of the martial qualities, e.g., the ability to bear the loss of the life of the husband (or son) remained. Also while discipline and toughness were required of the man, similar qualities had to be held to some extent by woman as well. The army is essentially hierarchical; nevertheless there is a strong sense of cooperative action and mutual support. To some extent these values have been fostered in Sikh women as well, and fit in rather well with the Sikh ethos as it has developed.

To summarise this discussion of the status and position of woman according to Sikh faith and tradition, one has to take note of many different factors and forces that have contributed to it in the past and continue to do so today. The pre-Sikh tradition in the Punjab area was essentially patriarchal, but in a somewhat natural and non-oppressive manner, at least psychologically. Punjab stands at the border of India. It has been historically the area of confluence of different cultural-racial streams, and social relations have tended on the whole to remain in a state of flux or at least flexibility. Thus, the various customs and traditions that the Sikh Gurus criticised, e.g. Sattee, are illustrated by what generally happened outside the Punjab region. It may be fair to say that even the status of woman did not become as established in the region as it did in parts of India that are farther removed from the periphery in the northwest. But the area was the right place for the Bhakti tradition to strike deeper roots than anywhere else in India, with the possible exception of another preripheral region, namely Assam. Sikhism not merely articulated the continuous flux that the Punjabi society experienced but gave it an appropriate ethos: the oneness and unity of man and the devine, even in the form of Guru-disciple relationship, enabled one to look at and deal with the worldly problems with confidence and a sense of responsibility. Applied to the status of women, this meant that household duties, specially the bearing of children, were ennobled. There was a divine touch to everything that happened and had to be done on this earth. Whether the work was that of a woman or a man, regardless of class of caste, it all partook of the sacred. Hence *Seva* or service became a prime element in Sikh practice. In that sense there was "equality" of all, women and men, high and low, because there was pride in all work.

The status of women was not an issue in Sikhism. Equality was implicit. Thus, at one point Guru Nanak says that if circumcision is a precondition for being a Muslim, then apparently women cannot become Muslim. Interestingly, this issue was not raised in the Islamic hagiography, but apparently it was important for Guru Nanak that women should be able to follow a faith. Women are considered as an integral part of society who must not be excluded by any ritual or doctrinal consideration. Since rituals tend to be exclusive, they cannot be made part of a true faith. In other words, the position of women could be a touchstone for the genuineness of a faith.

In Assam the Vaishnavite-bhakti doctrine of Sri Sankradeva has remained essentially unaltered to this day. But Punjab is ever in flux and confrontation with the dominant socio-political powers of India (from which Assam was cut off geopolitically to a considerable extent) has led to the transformation of Sikhism into a militant faith, and this transformation was consummated by the tenth Guru, Guru Gobind Singh. In the sociology of politics it is recognised that when a society becomes militaristic or oriented to defence-preparedness or aggression, the position of women tends to decline because they cannot play the role of armed warriors. But, as one notices in Assam where the sense of their status is treated by women as natural, rather than legal or ideological, the division of labour in society—such as the role of men as warriors or as leaders of militant mass movements—is not regarded by women as derogatory to their status. A similar attitude seems to have been adopted by women during the transformation of Sikhism into a militant faith. The men were fighting and dying; women were helping them and contributing their share. Certainly, no *macho* attitude towards women seems to have developed during this period of Sikh history, even if it seems to have crept in when feudalism began and some Sikh states developed. In other words, the macho male aggressiveness develops when the militancy becomes disfunctional and seeks other outlets as well as continued recognition. Nor did the macho tendencies gain acceptance by women in Sikhism because of the legacy of Guru Nanak and the high respect in which the Guru's female relatives were held by all, the Gurus themselves and their followers.

At the level of ultimate divinity, all distinctions vanish, even that between the divine power and the humans; the distinctions of sex also become irrelevant. At the worldly level different persons must perform different duties, but these do not create status differences, even though there may be functional distinctions of superiority, etc. A lurking identity of sameness underlies functional differences among the Sikhs, which makes them somewhat democratic, if not anarchistic, in their attitudes but also prevents the formation of stable organisations or institutional structures. Within this broad perspective, the status of women in the Sikh communities is today again in a state of flux and transition. Academic and technological specialisation as well as the growing affluence among the rural and urban strata produce a certain sense of crisis among the women as indeed also among men. How it turns out in the coming years remains to be seen.

CHAPTER XII

Buddhism from the Scriptural Point of View Emphasising the Status of Women

S. RANGASWAMY**

The Buddha once compared his teaching to a great ocean. "As the great ocean has but one taste, the taste of salt, so has this Dhamma but one taste, that of freedom". This freedom is called Nibbana—freedom from suffering—immortality. Nibbana is the ultimate focal point of topics dealt with in the *Tripitaka*. Thus the question of the Buddhist scriptures in relation to women must necessarily begin with the mention of those exalted women who walking on the Path indicated by the Buddha, had achieved the *Sumums Bonum*. An entire book of the Scriptures, the *Therigatha* (the Psalm of the Sisters) refers to such worthy women. The book records the inspired utterances made by those saintly nuns after their enlightenment. Since these utterances had the subsequent approval of the Buddha, the *Therigatha* bear the seal of the 'word of the Buddha'.

The magnificent personality of the Buddha and the brilliance of His teaching created such a stir in the country that it attracted a massive following, which included a large number of women from all walks of life.We will recount a few incidents described in the Buddhist scripture.

a) *Bhikkhuni Sangha.* Women held a position of subservience and were excluded from this or that worldly occupation or religious education. The establishment of the Order of Buddhist Nuns gave women an opportunity for spiritual practice and unfoldment. And this opportunity was eagerly taken advantage of, often with remarkable success.

b) *Law of Karma.* Woman's role as mother commanded veneration, but society generally expected her to give birth to a son, so that he could perform rituals for the salvation of his ancestors. Women were always in fear of the condemnation they would face if the baby happened to be a girl. So the

---

* S.Rangaswamy is a retired Wing Commander in the Indian Air Force

women engaged themselves in hectic prayers and going round the trees. The Law of Karma, 'as you saw, so you reap' was made the main issue of the teaching of the Buddha, and this refuted the efficacy of the rituals. It declared that the ancestors fare according to their desert, and not on the performance of rituals by the sons. Many women were relieved of the anxiety about the birth of a baby. It also said that family lineage could continue through daughters too. King Pasenadi was disappointed when Queen Mallika gave birth to a daughter. The Buddha said, "A woman child, O king, may prove even a better offspring than a male. For she may grow up wise and virtuous. The child she may bear may do great deeds, and rule great realm, yea, such a son of a noble wife becomes his country's guide".

c) *Unmarried women*. Some women seeking freedom from the drudgery and meaninglesness of life, and desiring to gain higher spiritual experience preferred to remain unmarried. But an unmarried woman had always been looked down upon by society. The Order of Buddhist Nuns was a boon to such women. It was thus that Subha became a nun.

d) *Bhadda Kundalakesi*. She was so intelligent that she was able to hold a meaningful debate with the Buddha's chief disciple, the Venerable Sariputta. Subsequently, she heard a discourse given by the Buddha, and that was sufficient to effect her enlightenment. Hers was a rare case of one becoming an *Arahat* before being ordained in the Order.

e) *Prakati*. Besides being a woman, she suffered the handicap of caste. When Venerable Ananda approached her at a well, and asked for water to drink, she was taken aback. "How can I give you water, sir? I am a Matanga". To this Venerable Ananda replied, "I ask for water, sister. I am not curious about your caste". Being accustomed to being treated as an outcaste, it was a novel experience for Pakati to be treated as a human being. It is no wonder that she took refuge in the Buddha.

f) *Family prosperity*. Women might bring prosperity to a family. "All families that have attained great possessions have done so for one of the following reasons: they search for what is lost, repair what is dilapidated, eat and drink in moderation, and place in authority a virtuous man or woman".

g) *Women in general*. Regarding most women, it is said, "A woman's goal is man, her ambition is for adornment, her resolve is for a child, her desire is to be without a rival, her fulfilment is authority".

h) *Happy married life*. The Buddha liked marriages to be happy. If husband and wife share the same beliefs, ethical behaviour, generosity and wisdom, they with have a happy marriage.

'Therefore girls, train yourselves thus: 'To whatever husband our parents shall give us, for him we will rise up early, be the last to retire, be willing workers, order all things sweetly and speak affectionately. Train yourselves thus, girls.

"And in this way too, girls: we will honour and respect all whom our husbands honour and respect, whether mother or father, recluse or Brahmin, and on their arrival offer them water and a seat.

"And in this way too, girls, we will be deft and nimble at our husbands's home-crafts, whether they be of wool or cotton, making it our business to understand the work so to do it and get it done. Train yourselves thus, girls. And in this way too, girls, whatever our husbands' households consist of — servants and messenger and work people — we will know the work of each one of them, what has been done, and their remissions by way of what has not been done: we will know the strengths and weaknesses of the sick; we will portion out the food fairly. Train yourselves thus, girls. And in this way too, girls, the treasure, grain, silver and gold that our husbands bring home we will keep safely, acting as no robber or spend-thrift in regard to it. Train yourselves thus, girls"

If all goes well, then the wife is called the 'comrade supreme' and a number of devoted couples are mentioned in the *Pali Canon*.

One ideally matched pair was Nakula-Pita and Nakula-Mata. "Neither is aware of having transgressed against the other in thought, much less in person, and each expresses the longing to be together not only here and now but in the future state also. The Buddha reassures them on this point, and gives as his reason that both of them are on the same level in regard to their belief, their ethical conduct, their generosity and wisdom. In these respects therefore a woman may be the equal of a man.

i) *The Power of the Vajjians.* King Pasenadi of Kosala had planned a military compaign against the Vijjian Republic, and he went to the Buddha to seek his blessings. In the presence of the king the Buddha put several questions to Ananda and he answered all of them in the affirmative. Then, in each case, the Buddha pronounced the Truth. One such question referred to women. "Do the Vijjians treat their women with honour, O Lord?" was the question. Then the Buddha declared, "The men who do not maltreat their women, but treat them with respect will have better lives and not decline". What the Buddha tried to impress on the king was that the noble quality which the Vijjians possessed constituted an invincible power. The king gave up the idea of attacking the Vajjians.

Glorious history. Numerous other such incidents could be cited from the *Tripitaka*. But what does all this mean? It means that in those days the status of women in India was such that they suffered a variety of handicaps. This suffering was neither more nor less than their suffering in earlier times. But during the dispensation of the Buddha, their status appears to have taken a quantum jump. This is all part of a glorious history and mangnificent heritage. The glorious history should be studied (a) to create awe and admiration for that glory and thus (b) to stimulate one to take purposive action in the present. If the second action is not fulfilled, the study of history becomes a useless gloating over a dead past. Heritage, to be meaningful, has to be dynamic. It would therefore be profitable to see what guidelines for present action can be derived from the *Pali Canon*.

a) When we hold hold consultations about the status of women, it means that their present status is not good enough. They are unhappy. So, improving their status means making them happy. The highest form of happiness is Nibbana, and this is the happiness Buddha gave to his disciples. Can we too give our women this happiness? There may be some women who would very much like to get away from it all — even away from a preferred status.

b) Most women seek worldly happiness only and not Nibbàna. So let it be clearly understood that worldly happiness can never be unalloyed. In the world of phenomenal existence, women (and also men) have always suffered, suffer now, and will suffer in the future. But even in this dismal state, there is room for well-meaning people to act and effect a modicum of improvement in the status of women. And this has to be done.

c) 'First Comprehension' is the clear comprehension of the goal. For this, one has to be very clear about the unsatisfactoriness of the status of women, and what is desired to be achieved. The attainment of the goal may be in phases, with intermediate goals. All human problems are inter-linked in some way. The problems have a tendency to gang up to frustrate solution. So the problems of women should be broken up into minute parts and each one tackled separately.

d) 'Second Comprehension'. There should be clear comprehension about the method to be adopted for achieving the goal. There may be several methods but the best one has to be selected. The right method is one that has no adverse side-effects and produces lasting results.

e) An effort to improve the status of woman should not degenerate into a fight for equality with men, for it will only lead to confrontation, rivalry and competition. Despite equality it must be remembered that woman is fundamentally different from man. The Buddha lays great stress on the complementary nature of their personalities, which forms a beautiful human relationship. A powerful weapon in the women's armoury is her feminity, and this should not be jeopardised.

f) Internal-External. The deficiency in the status of women may have internal or external causes. That is to say women themselves are responsible for some of their miseries. These areas should be identified and corrected first.

g) Sila or morally upright behaviour is the foundation of all spiritual endeavour. A truly high status can be gained by a women only when her character is of a high quality.

h) Harmonious development is necessary. The baby may need a wash, but the baby should not be thrown away with the bath-water.

i) Causes. Every problem has its causes. Wisdom lies in correctly identifying and eliminating the causes. With the cause gone the problem goes. If a remedial action does not touch the cause, the so-called remedial action is just a ritual.

j) The blind cannot lead the blind. One who is going to lead women to a higher status must herself/himself have a status to do so.

There should be no discrepancy between what the leader says, does and thinks. One having a discrepancy is a hypocrite. The motivating factor should be compassion.

k) All women are not equally amenable to upliftment. A wise farmer will chose the most fertile field for cultivation. Similarly it may be advisable to determine priorities in selecting areas for action for advancement of women.

l) Decay is the law of nature. Everything decays including a success in the upliftment of women. Unless what is gained is consolidated and maintained by constant vigilance the gain will soon be lost.

CHAPTER XIII

Status of Women in Buddhism

N.D. KAMBLE*

Women were believed to be weaker than men and by virtue of their being women were handicapped. Therefore, in the course of time, men made them take the shelter of men. By habit and customs women were given lower status by various social groups, in different parts of the world. Of late, religions and faiths have also adopted the then-existing social norms.

In India, Vedic religion and then Hindu religion, gave inferior status to women as compared to men. For example, *Smiritis* like *Manusmiriti*, *Gautam Smriti* and other scriptures categorically stated that a woman has to be under supervision and guidance throughout her life; during her childhood under the supervision of her father, during youth under the supervision of her husband and during old age under the supervision of her son.

Buddhism did not indicate such a dictum, on the contrary it treated women on a par with men for all practical purposes, except for those differences due to nature.

In most of the religions women were not allowed to even hear religious hymns. In fact, in Vedic religion women and Sudras were treated as impure, hence unfit to perform any religious function. Whereas in Buddhism, not only were women were allowed to hear the religious discourses but were also allowed to participate in them and were also allowed to give religious discourses. Thus, the status of a Buddhist woman in the religion was quite high compared to Vedic/Hindu religion and Muslim religion.

Women were prohibited from learning in the Vedic faith, while in Buddhism not only were women allowed to learn but were also allowed to teach religion. In Muslim religion, the women were a non-existing entity.

---

* Professor in the Institute for Social and Economic Change, Bangalore.

The highest order in religion is the monkhood, which is attained mainly by men in Hindu and Muslim religions but in Buddhism many women become monks and many of them preached.

The highest honour one could get in religion was to be a monk or priest or a religious teacher. Such honour was never conferred on women in other religions. But there are many examples of women monks and priests in Buddhism.

Socially privileged men and not women could become religious leaders in the religions. But in Buddhism even socially under privileged men could become priests, like Sopaka, Angulimals, Sokpal, Asang etc., and women like Sujatha. The status of women was not determined by birth, but was determined by worth in Buddhism unlike other religions where birth is the determinant of not only the status of the woman but also of all her activities during her life time. In the Hindu religion, a woman is born in a particular caste and follows all rituals and dictums meant for women in that particular caste. Status thus attached to her does not disappear even after her death. Thus status in the Hindu fold is fixed and unchangeably assigned to women while in Buddhism even Lord Buddha did not discriminate between women and men while giving his sermons. Both men and women were allowed to participate in his sermons. He not only gave equal treatment to men and women, but also permitted women to learn and even to teach religious scripts to others. Normally this privilege is given to men from only privileged sections of the society in other religions. But in Buddhism, Buddha allowed women to use robes meant for monks. During those days, the status of the monk was the highest possible social privilege. It was approved and accepted by the then existing society. This was because of the acceptance of the higher social status of woman in Buddhism and the equal treatment they were given with men unlike other religions and faiths.

Unlike other religions, in Buddhism women were allowed to participate in debates, discussions and were even permitted to deliver judgements as found in many *Jathakas* relating to *Janapathas*. *Janapathas* were like city republics where both adult men and women were given equal rights in most of the social activities including panchayats, politics, judiciary and religions. Unfortunately it was not followed by other religions because the status of women was lower in other religions.

Because their status was lower in other religions the attempts of women for their liberation became futile both in east and west. Even in family matters, the word of women is not taken seriously, because of the belief that they are incapable of doing any good thing. But there is no question of their attainments in public life. There are many examples of women scholars in Buddhism like Sangamithra and others who with their scholarship and wisdom defeated well known religious scholars in Buddhism, Vedic religion and Jainism. Even Negasena, the great scholar and Buddhist monk, who convinced Milind and Great, had many discussions with women Buddhist scholars during his mission. All these things happened when women in most other religions were treated as non-existent.

Therefore, for better status and equality for women, Buddhism is the best religion.

CHAPTER XIV

Women In Zorastrianism

DASTOOR N.D. MINOCHEHR-HOMJI
and
DEENAZ DAMANIA

A) Women in Zorastrian Literature

"We esteem and revere the virtuous woman, richer in Good Thoughts, richer in Kind Words and richer in Truthful Deeds, well accomplished, Sovereign over her Time and Leisure, Virtuous, like Spentas Aaramaiti, the Queen of womanly Ideal, and such as are Thy feminine aspects, O Mazda", e.g. Aban, Ashish-Vanguhi, Daenaa, and Paarendi (the genious of keen Intelligence)! (*Aiwisroothrem Geh* !V,para 9, S.B.E.Vol.31,386)

The word for "woman", in *Avesta*, is *genaa*, *naairikaa* and *kainikaa* (maiden).

From the above quotation, we know clearly the 'standing' women had in ancient Iranian society. The reference to her receiving an all-round education points to her equality in society, as an elightened member of the family. She is likened to Amramati, a feminine supreme attribute of Ahura Mazda, that represents the characteristic Power of Discrimination (*vikeka*), enabling one to exercise the proper perspective of values, and discrimination between right and wrong. Among other feminine aspects (*genaa*) are: (a) Anaahitaa or Aabaan which represents Moral Purity and Lustre, consequent upon the former. *Aabaan* Nyaish expounds this concept of Moral Purity in unmistakable terms. (b) *Daena* or *Deen* represents Religion, Religious Life and Conscience, the seat of Religious and Moral life. Daena represents, moreover, the Profound Vision on the path of Life. (c) *Ashish* Vanguhi is Bliss or Blessedness consequent upon a moral and virtuous life. She represents the wealth of virtues not of temporal riches.The close associate of Ashish Vanguhi is Paarendi, Quick Intelligence, treading the narrow path of Virtue (*rao-rathaa*).

A note of warning is necessary here; the western scholars, like L.H. Mills and others, render '*genaao*' as the *wives* of Ahura Mazda ! Ustad Cawasjee Kanga renders it as the feminine aspects of Ahura Mazda, represented by Spandaarmad, Abaan, Deen, Ashish Vangh (&Marespand).

The seven sisters of Ardaa Viraf have been known to recite holy manthras before their saintly brother when he lay in a trance. The Iranian woman could even work as a priest as can be gathered from *Aerpatastaan & Nirangastaan* (I-i.5 *Sacred Books of the East*, Vol. IV, p. 307). She could work as a judge (*S.B.E.*, Vol. XXXVII p. 80). This is really heartening and edifying to note, in an age when even the witness of a women was doubted! In the *Avesta* references to men and women are remembered with equal reverence: In the quotation with which the article begins, the woman (*nairikaamcha ashaoneem*) is remembered reverently first and then secondly the 'virtuous men' (*naremcha ashavanem*). In the small but beautiful Younhey Haataam prayer, both men and women ever endeavouring to ascend in dignity of being are reverently remembered. We reproduce below our interpretation of the prayer:

Life's better and Superior, By good Deeds cum fervent Prayer!

By Truth does Mazda measure Man's Merit !

I esteem, with love and reverence the Souls endeavouring to rise.

And endeavouring myself likewise,

'In dignity of being I ascend' !

The reverence for woman catches our eye when we study *Ferverdin* (XIII) *Yasht:* The whole of the *Kerdeh* XXX is devoted to the roll of honour, inscribed to Wise and Virtuous (*ashava vidhwaao*) Woman (paras 139-142: *S.B.E.* vol. XXIII pp.224-226).

Ashishvang Yaskt (XVIII) paras 57-59 (*S.B.E.*, Vol., XXIII, P. 281), depict the spirit of Womanhood, viz. Ashi, bewailing the three unfortunate situations in which a woman is placed by morally unscrupluous men: (a) a demi-monde, who practised abortion, (b) the greater moral blemish of a woman who conceived outside of marital relations and tried to present the issue as her own husband's! and (c) the State and the social agency who neglect to settle girls of marriageable age.

Lastly, both boys and girls undergo the sacrament of Navjote, without any difference. Our ancestors reverenced the women in society, for they believed firmly in the Tennysonian statement:

"For woman is not an underdeveloped man,

Nor yet man's opposite ! "

B)Parsi Women's Status in Society Today

What is the socio-cultural status of the Parsi woman today and what are the factors that have contributed to her present status? I shall approach this question by discussing the various indices by which social status can be judged.

1.The Level of Education

The Parsi woman's formal education rarely stops at high school level. Parents put a high premium on education — whether of a girl or a boy. Parental aspirations and ambitions are equally high for children of both sexes. Small families of 1 or 2 children ensures, generally, that each child is valued as an individual.

2.The Level of Economic Independence

Due to generally higher levels of education, the Parsi woman works in jobs which are fairly well-paid. For some reason at the moment secretarial jobs are popular, and with efficiency and integrity women have built up a good rapport at work and carved out a special niche for themselves. Women in different professions have put in a lot of hard work and distinguished themselves. Education coupled with economic independence, has been the key to the Parsi woman's emancipation. But therein also lies her dilemma. Sometimes the important need for having a home and children is sacrificed in favour of economic independence and self-employment.

a) Due to the greater number of years spent in education, marriages are delayed to the late twenties.

b) Once a woman has enjoyed a certain salary level in her own right, she starts expecting her man to earn more and this has created a serious problem in her ability to find a mate.

c) Delayed childbearing: Most Parsi couples today, have only one or two children and this has resulted in a negative population growth. Ten years ago, there was one Parsi for every 4,800

Indians. Today, there is one Parsi for every 8,000 Indians.The world-wide Parsi population is placed between 1,14,000 and 1,20,000. Only about 90,000 live in India, mostly in Bombay. Bombay owes a major part of its early growth, from a mere fishing village to the centre of commerce and industry and education that it is today, to the Parsis. This tremendous problem of dwindling numbers and terribly tiny population size, is a cause of great anxiety.

3.The Power of Decision-making in the Home and Outside

In the average Parsi marriage, the woman enjoys equal decision-making authority with the husband. In fact there are jokes about the Parsi woman being a very domineering and assertive person. She generally holds strong views and opinions which she unhesitatingly shares !

Due to their civic mindedness and readiness to espouse worthy social causes, Parsi women have been in the foreground of many organisations such as Beauty Without Cruelty, the World Wildlife Fund, the Western India Automobile Association, etc. In fact, even before Independence was achieved by India, the first Indian flag was hoisted by a Parsi woman in Germany, where she was actively fighting on India's behalf.

4.Development of a Positive Self-Concept

The Parsi girl is hardly ever made to feel second best. Our prophet Zarathushtra, in the *Gathas*, has laid stress over and over on the equality of man and woman in every sphere of life. Ahura Mazda, the Zoroastrian concept of God, has been described in terms of Six Attributes: three male and three female. The Good Mind, Moral Strength, and Righteousness are the male attributes, whereas, True Devotion, Perfection, and Immortality are the female attributes.

Sociologists have told us that feelings of inferiority, of being second best which become part of a woman's psyche, from the time she is in her cradle, get repressed as she gets older, but affect her behaviour in adulthood. A lot of us women are termed 'martyrs' —we like to suffer. This is aggression turned against oneself — self-directed feelings of anger, possibly due to early rejection, unfavourable comparisons with boys, etc. The Parsi female child generally escapes this kind of early traumatic feeling of not being wanted. As an adult she has a fairly positive self image, and confident outlook on life.

In spite of the special position she enjoys in her community, the Parsi woman does not enjoy equal status in other areas.

The Problem of Children of Mixed marriages

When a Parsi man marries outside his faith, his children have the right to follow Zoroastrianism. When a Parsi woman marries a man of another faith, she and her children are considered lost to the community, and can never follow their mother's religion. This practice denies the community some of its legitimate population. This has been defended saying that ours is a patriarchal society and therefore when a woman marries outside the community she should be perfectly ready to forego her rights and privileges as a Parsi woman. More serious thought needs to be given to this situation as it exists. Are we justified in following one set of rules for the man, and another for the woman? Other patriarchal societies like the Hindus, Mulsims, Christians, Jews have not denied this right to the woman.

Also in general, eminent lawyers of the community have strongly felt the need for reform in the Parsi Marriage and Divorce Act, and the Law of Succession, both of which were enacted in the last century. The woman's position needs to be properly safeguarded.